Patriots of Two Nations

Patriots of Two Nations

Why Trump Was Inevitable
And What Happens Next

Spencer Critchley

McDavid Media
Carmel, California

Published in the United States of America
by McDavid Media
Carmel, California
www.mcdavid.media

www.spencercritchley.com
ISBN: 979-8635466575

For Lila

ACKNOWLEDGMENTS

Thank you to Vinz Koller, for suggesting I get involved in politics; Plasha Fielding Will for showing me the ropes; former Congressman Sam Farr for showing me there are good people serving in elected office; Zach Friend for always living up to his last name; Connie Davis and all at the Canadian Broadcasting Corporation who taught me how communication works; music for teaching me how communication can work in other ways; Michael Blake, Brent Colburn, Amy Chapman, Kevin Lewis, and all at Obama for America for inspiring me so much and giving me a bigger family; my Boots Road Group partner Lynne Weatherman and all the Boots Roadies; and Lila Critchley for being there when I looked up.

Thank you to Lila, Jason Warburg, Wendy Davis Johnson, Beth Charlton, Susan Arcady Barich, David Delp, and Terence Elliott for careful, perceptive, and helpful readings.

If a lion could talk, we would not be able to understand him.

— *Ludwig Wittgenstein*

Only connect.

— *E.M. Forster*

Contents

Introduction: Election Night..1

Part 1 How We Got Here 5

The Two Nations...7
A New World 9
The Counter-Enlightenment 12
What Is a Nation?..18
The Battle Between & Within 23
"The Center Cannot Hold" 30
"Print the Legend"...33
His Majesty the Baby 38
The Map Begins to Tear..43
The Global Elite 49
A Virtual Secession...52
We're Throwing Our Own Party..57
When Everyone Is Out to Get You 60
Enter the Demagogue 63

Part II What's Happening Now 67

Trump Was Inevitable...69
Liberals: Good at Economics, Bad at Culture 72
Culture & Soul 76
Poetry, Magic & Amusement 80
There Are Two Kinds of Truth...88
Status & Survival 94
Meritocracy & Corruption: How Wrong Can Look Right 97
The Evolution of Tribalism 100
The Culture of Tribalism: Blood, Soil & Loyalty 104
Identity Politics 108
The Problem of Evil: When Cruelty Is the Point...115
Beyond Evil: The Hollow Men 120
The State of the Union & the State of Our Minds...126

Part III What's Next 135

Restoration or Retribution? 137
Stop Making Sense..142
Across the Great Divide 148
America Is More Than an Idea...158
Afterword, 2020: Campaigns Are Not Logical, but Mythological.................159

About the Author..164
Endnotes...166

Introduction:
Election Night

On Nov. 8, 2016, I was at a hotel in Phoenix, Arizona, at a party I had helped organize for the Hillary Clinton campaign. Like everyone else there and at similar gatherings across the country, I assumed we were about to celebrate Hillary's election as the next President of the United States.

It wasn't that Hillary had run a great campaign — far from it. That's why I was there. I had flown to Phoenix just eight days before to help with media relations, social media, photography, and anything else I could contribute, including setting up the stage and wrangling reporters at this party.

Like many people who had worked on previous Democratic presidential campaigns, I had planned to sit this one out, figuring I wouldn't be needed. On paper if not on the stump, Hillary was one of the most qualified candidates in history. Her opponent looked to us like one of the *least* qualified in history — and he himself seemed to assume Hillary would win.

Donald Trump was a real estate promoter and TV personality with a bad reputation in his home city of New York and no experience in government. He had built his political profile by exploiting a racist conspiracy theory about Barack Obama's birth certificate. He had campaigned on xenophobia and an evident contempt for democratic norms and institutions. He had invested little money or effort in his run and appeared to see it as a brand-building exercise.

But as Election Day had approached, I had started to get nervous, and so had others like me. We called up friends on the campaign, asking, "Can I help?"

The answer should have been, "Nah, we got this." It wasn't.

"Yes, can you come now?"

And so here I was, volunteering alongside veterans with experience going back to Bill Clinton's campaigns.

Still, she *had* to win, right? How could she not? That didn't make any sense.

And then Ohio was called for Trump. And then Florida. And then the world turned upside down.

On Election Night 2008, at an Obama campaign party, I had cried tears of joy. It wasn't just because my side had won. It was because I believed the whole country had won, no matter how they had voted, because of the inspiring values Obama stood for and — as his campaign staff knew well — lived by.

I cried in 2016 too, for very different reasons. But across the street, the Arizona Republicans were holding *their* election night party. From there, I heard a rising roar of exultation.

On my side of the street, it was close to silent. Almost no one felt up to talking to the media. I happened to take a call from the Australian Broadcasting Corporation. I couldn't begin to explain what had just happened — how had the same country that had elected an Obama now elected a demagogue?

A few days later, I tried again, by writing a piece for the Huffington Post (now HuffPost) called "A Letter to a Friend Who Voted for Trump."[1] In it, I addressed, anonymously, a person I knew to be good, honest, and patriotic, asking him to help me understand what could lead him, like millions of others, to make this choice.

I've been working on understanding that every day, ever since. Along the way I've studied not just where we are now, but how we got here, going back to the founding of the United States.

This book is the result.

I believe I now do understand what happened. What led us to 2016 was bigger, and had deeper roots, than any of us realized, or than has been reported elsewhere.

The election of Donald Trump should not have been a shock. Whether he came along in 2016 or a little later, Trump, or someone like him, was inevitable.

And yet most of us were blindsided by his victory, and few yet see the full scope of what it means. Understanding how and why Trump won — including how *all of us* helped make it happen — is critical to our future as a democracy.

In these pages, I'll show how our history has led us, inexorably, to this present. I'll show what I believe is coming next. And I'll offer some hope for how, if we can meet the true challenge of this moment, it might work out for the better.

Part 1

How We Got Here

The Two Nations

I n any democracy, we expect political division. But what America is going through during the presidency of Donald Trump feels more like a Cold Civil War. The opposing sides don't just disagree over the issues. Each views the other as a threat to the country.

And yet both Trump supporters and Trump opponents see themselves as patriots. How can that be?

They are patriots of two nations.

These two nations occupy one territory, but their people live in different worlds. Even if they speak the same language, the words they use refer to different perceptions and different ways of understanding those perceptions. They hold different values. They even have different ways of defining what's true and what's false.

For all these reasons, arguments between members of the two nations often have been a waste of time, or have made the division even deeper.

But that division is far from new. The two nations have co-existed in tension, and sometimes combat, since the creation of the United States.

The Founders believed that they had designed a new *kind* of nation, one built not on tribal identity or conquest, but on reason. In so doing, they would set history on a new course.

But declaring it so did not make it so — not then and, as we're discovering two and half centuries later, not now.

In a 1991 speech at the Hoover Institution, former British Prime Minister Margaret Thatcher captured in a few phrases the historical singularity that is America:

No other nation has been built upon an idea—the idea of liberty. No other nation has so successfully combined people of different races and nations within a single culture. Both the founding fathers of the United States and successive waves of immigrants to your country were determined to create a new identity… The European nations are not and can never be like this. They are the product of history and not of philosophy.[2]

Thatcher spoke at the pinnacle of the American Century, when American democracy appeared triumphant. What she did not see, and what almost no one saw then, was how tenuous that triumph was.

Both America and democracy itself had been built on a foundation that had never been solid, and which was now beginning to buckle.

We have never fully understood what divided us. We saw that race did — slavery was our original sin. We saw that economics did — despite our American dream of a classless society, money still mattered.

But there was more, so much more that we couldn't see it, because it's hard to see reality itself. And the reality experienced in one of our two nations is not the same as the reality experienced in the other.

Messages between them can make perfect sense when sent, and no sense when received.

Until we learn to connect across that great divide, we have not finished creating the United States.

A New World

The American Revolution began as a revolution in thought. The American Revolutionaries were people of the Enlightenment, an era named for a new dawn of awareness. The Renaissance had seen the rediscovery of ancient knowledge. The Age of Reason brought tools for the discovery of new knowledge. The Enlightenment marked a new way of knowing. Evidence and logic began to take precedence over revelation and religion. Reason overthrew faith as the ultimate source of authority.

With the birth of the United States of America, reason overthrew a king, and the divine right that had granted him power.

Both reason and faith had always been aspects of human thought, but throughout previous history, faith had dominated, though not without challenge. While their fellow Greeks tended the temples of capricious gods, the philosophers of ancient Athens devoted themselves to reason, forming ideas that would inspire our Founders many centuries later. Socrates argued that society should be ruled by philosopher kings, as recounted by Plato in *The Republic*:

> Neither cities nor States nor individuals will ever attain
> perfection until the small class of philosophers whom we
> termed useless but not corrupt are providentially compelled,
> whether they will or not, to take care of the State.[3]

At the cost of his own life, Socrates' advocacy for reason would influence Western thought ever after. But as Judaism and then Christianity rose in reach and power, Jerusalem took over as the symbolic seat of authority. "What has Jerusalem to do with Athens?" asked the early Christian writer Tertullian.[4]

From the latter days of Rome, through the Dark Ages, the Middle Ages, and the Renaissance, Jerusalem prevailed — often by force. Christian philosophers such as Augustine, Abelard, and Aquinas used reason to guide their thinking, but the source, always, was revelation. To claim to discover new truths was heresy, punishable by excommunication, torture, or death.

It wasn't until nearly 2,000 years after Socrates that the supremacy of faith would face another significant challenge, when science enabled humans to trespass on domains previously reserved for God. In 1543, Nicolaus Copernicus used mathematics and astronomy to study the "revolutions of the celestial spheres" — and discovered that the Earth was not the center of the universe. In his *Discourse on Method* of 1637, René Descartes used human perception, not divine revelation, as the source of what we know: "I think, therefore I am." By 1687, Isaac Newton was able to perceive how the universe moved, and explained it in his *Principia Mathematica*.

America was among a rush of other scientific discoveries. Science produced the tools that enabled Europeans to find this "New World," and the nation they created there was founded on scientific principles.

Although many of the original colonists were religious pilgrims, the authors of the Declaration of Independence and the Constitution were inspired by Enlightenment thinkers such as Locke, Montesquieu, Rousseau, and Voltaire, who in turn had built on the scientific breakthroughs of the Age of Reason. Freedom was "the firstborn daughter of science," wrote Thomas Jefferson, in a 1795 letter.[5] Equality and self-rule were embedded in scientific "natural law."

The "self-evident" truths stated in the Declaration echoed Locke's *Second Treatise of Government*. Here is Locke:

> Whensoever therefore the legislative… by ambition, fear, folly
> or corruption, endeavour to grasp themselves, or put into the
> hands of any other, an absolute power over the lives, liberties,
> and estates of the people… they forfeit the power the people
> had put into their hands… and it devolves to the people, who
> have a right to resume their original liberty, and, by the
> establishment of a new legislative… provide for their own
> safety and security.[6]

And here is Jefferson's language in the Declaration:

> We hold these truths to be self-evident, that all men are created
> equal, that they are endowed by their Creator with certain

unalienable Rights, that among these are Life, Liberty and the pursuit of Happiness.—That to secure these rights, Governments are instituted among Men, deriving their just powers from the consent of the governed,—That whenever any Form of Government becomes destructive of these ends, it is the Right of the People to alter or to abolish it.[7]

Jefferson substituted "happiness" for Locke's "estates of the people," or property. That points to a key difference between what would become the liberal and conservative views of freedom: liberals tend to be wary of influence derived from private property, while conservatives see property rights and individual rights as inextricably linked. That difference persists to this day, but as we'll see, its significance has paled in comparison to others.

The Founders did not make a clean break with faith. To varying degrees, they all seem to have held to religious or at least spiritual beliefs — Jefferson may have been a deist, for example. In writing the First Amendment to the Constitution, they not only limited the role of religion, they protected religious freedom.

But in asserting natural rights of liberty, equality, and self-rule, they asserted that reason had finally triumphed in the long struggle between two ways of seeing, understanding, and acting in the world.

It turned out they had performed a secular miracle. The American experiment would succeed beyond any dream of history and become a model for all free nations.

Because our history is written on that success, we tend to assume that the success was complete, that the Enlightenment, as instantiated in the United States of America, defined the course of the modern world. As the upstart Americans had defeated the British Empire, so the new world had defeated the old.

But the old world never agreed to the terms of surrender.

The Counter-Enlightenment

As the Enlightenment began, so too did a resistance movement: the Counter-Enlightenment. Though it has often been overlooked, that resistance continues to this day.

The conflict between the two is now tearing us apart.

Throughout America's history, our failure to recognize and understand that conflict has prevented us from fulfilling the union's founding promise.

The Enlightenment and the Counter-Enlightenment are not just two competing philosophical systems. They are different worldviews. People who inhabit them see life differently, use language differently, and even define truth differently.

When we find ourselves arguing with people who seem to be in an alternate reality, it doesn't necessarily mean that they, or we, have gone crazy.

It may be that we *are* in alternate realities.

The vanguard of the Enlightenment were the French *philosophes,* led by Voltaire, who saw reason as the light of human progress. In most of today's world, that belief is nearly a truism, but in the 18th century, it was revolutionary.

But not everyone wanted this revolution — then or now. As the light of reason rose over the world, many people recoiled from what it revealed. Such resisters included theologians, monarchists, traditionalists, artists, and philosophers.

Some of them resisted because they saw a threat to their power, which had been based on faith and tradition. Some were poorly educated, and feared any threat to long-held beliefs. But many sincere, informed people believed that a world ruled by reason would be soulless and immoral. They saw that reason was necessary and useful. But they strove to save religion, poetry, tradition, rural life, and culture from "the dead hand of France," as the British philosopher Isaiah

Berlin described Enlightenment rationalism in a definitive 1973 essay, "The Counter-Enlightenment."

Most modern, educated Westerners grew up with the Enlightenment worldview as their default reality. That includes nearly all classical liberals (meaning people across the ideological spectrum who believe in democracy, the rule of law, and freedom) and it includes me. For us, it's easy to dismiss the Counter-Enlightenment as simple reaction by the old guard against the new, which is how I used to think of it. There is some obvious truth in this: A Counter-Enlightenment path can be tracked through reactionary movements ever since, including the worst of them, Nazism.

But any serious reading of Counter-Enlightenment thinking — a reading many of us will have missed during a typical, Enlightenment-based public education — reveals that it demands consideration. More, it now demands a response.

The Enlightenment *philosophes* believed, as Berlin describes, "that human nature was fundamentally the same in all times and places," that "human beings could be defined as a species, like animals, or plants, or minerals," and that therefore "methods similar to those of Newtonian physics, which had achieved such triumphs in the realm of inanimate nature, could be applied with equal success to the fields of ethics, politics and human relationships in general."[8]

Today, such assumptions are so familiar and widely accepted that they're like the air we breathe — if we live within the dominant Enlightenment worldview. We understand our lives and our society in terms of physics, biology, psychology, sociology, economics, and political science. But to Counter-Enlightenment thinkers, the belief that reason could explain so much was both mistaken and destructive.

The Italian political philosopher Giambattista Vico was little-known during his lifetime, which bridged the Age of Reason and the Enlightenment (he lived from 1668 to 1744). But in retrospect we can see that Vico was a prophet of the Counter-Enlightenment. In his *The New Science* (1725), Vico argued that science, as practiced by rationalists like the then-ascendant Descartes, was a closed, self-referential system, and, therefore, ultimately meaningless. Science only *seemed* to describe the world so accurately — because it excluded everything in the world that wasn't scientific.

In Vico's view, Descartes' philosophy substituted reduction for reality. Descartes had sought to rebuild knowledge from the ground up. He questioned everything he thought he knew and started over from that which could not be doubted, the apparently self-evident fact of his own existence: "I think, therefore I am." From that new starting point, he reasoned that we could trust other "clear and distinct ideas," in particular those that could be stated and tested mathematically.

The power of mathematics, especially in Descartes' hands, was clear at the time and of course is to this day, when it remains the foundation of science. But Vico insisted that mathematics could only address what was mathematical — in other words, itself. If you started with mathematical ideas, whether as simple as the concept of numbers, or as complex as Descartes' analytic geometry, then yes, mathematics could be used to say true things about them. The same held for logic: If something was logical, you could make logical statements about it.

But, Vico argued, we have no way of knowing what relationship mathematics and logic have to the reality beyond them. That was because a thing could only be fully understood, in its purpose and its meaning, by its maker. Humans had made mathematics, and so humans could understand mathematics. But humans had not made the universe — which is why its purpose and meaning are obscure to us. Only the one who had made the universe could understand it. That was God.

Reason shrank the universe to what could be understood with reason. Said Vico, "Man makes himself the measure of all things."[9] In his 18th century diction, he was one of the first to point out that when all you have is a hammer, everything looks like a nail: "Whenever men can form no idea of distant and unknown things, they judge them by what is familiar and at hand."[10]

Other thinkers of the time came to similar conclusions. The work of the influential German Lutheran philosopher Johann Georg Hamann made difficult reading, but that may have been deliberate. Hamann believed that if ideas were too tidy, they were probably wrong, because reality was too complex to be captured with logic alone. Instead, not logic but poetry was "the mother-tongue of the human race."[11] Himself a former rationalist who had converted to Christianity, Hamann asserted that an overarching trust in reason was itself a form of faith:

Being, belief and reason are pure relations, which cannot be
dealt with absolutely, and are not things but pure scholastic
concepts, signs for understanding, not for worshipping, aids to
awaken our attention, not to fetter it.[12]

In rejecting rationalism, many Counter-Enlightenment thinkers also doubted
objective truth, at least as it could be perceived by humans. Both experience and
truth, they argued, were inherently subjective. Far from sharing universal values,
or having "natural" rights, people were individuals, whose values and rights were
embedded in distinct cultures.

Berlin summarizes this perspective while discussing the German philosopher
Johann Gottfried von Herder:

For Herder… to belong to a given community… is a basic
human need no less natural than that for food or drink or
security or procreation. One nation can understand and
sympathise with the institutions of another only because it
knows how much its own mean to itself. Cosmopolitanism is
the shedding of all that makes one most human, most oneself…

Imitation of models… leads to artificiality, feeble
imitativeness, degraded art and life. Germans must be Germans
and not third-rate Frenchmen; life lies in remaining steeped in
one's own language, tradition, local feeling; uniformity is
death. The tree of (science-dominated) knowledge kills the tree
of life.[13]

Like Hamann and Herder, many Counter-Enlightenment figures were
ethnically (though not yet nationally) German. Many saw themselves as
protecting a mythology-infused German culture against the rationalist French.
They saw the French as the descendants of the brutally efficient Roman invaders
who had subjugated the innocent, harmonious culture of ancient Germania.

Despite the fundamental differences between the Enlightenment and
Counter-Enlightenment worldviews, not everyone belonged only to one or the
other. Jean-Jacques Rousseau was one who spanned them. Rousseau's social
contract theory (along with Locke's) was a keystone of the Enlightenment.[14] But
he also made strongly Counter-Enlightenment arguments against civilization

itself. He saw civilization as a fallen state of the "noble savage," as he argued in his "Discourse on the Origin of Inequality" (1754):

> The example of savages, most of whom have been found in this
> state, seems to prove that men were meant to remain in it, that
> it is the real youth of the world, and that all subsequent
> advances have been apparently so many steps towards the
> perfection of the individual, but in reality towards the
> decrepitude of the species.[15]

Fear of where the Enlightenment might lead rose with the coming of the American Revolution. It was confirmed by the French Revolution. The Irish politician and philosopher Edmund Burke responded with "Reflections on the Revolution in France" (1790), which would become a founding document of modern conservatism. Burke argued that science, and the social contract theory descended from it, could manage society only by deploying a cruelly inhuman reductionism and by abandoning the traditions that held people together:

> All the pleasing illusions, which made power gentle, and
> obedience liberal... are to be dissolved by this new conquering
> empire of light and reason. All the decent drapery of life is to
> be rudely torn off...
>
> The state ought not to be considered as nothing better than a
> partnership agreement in a trade of pepper and coffee, calico or
> tobacco, or some other such low concern, to be taken up for a
> little temporary interest, and to be dissolved by the fancy of the
> parties. It is to be looked on with other reverence; because it is
> not a partnership in things subservient only to the gross animal
> existence of a temporary and perishable nature. It is a
> partnership in all science; a partnership in all art; a partnership
> in every virtue, and in all perfection. As the ends of such a
> partnership cannot be obtained in many generations, it becomes
> a partnership not only between those who are living, but
> between those who are living, those who are dead, and those
> who are to be born.[16]

But there was no going back. With the creation of the United States of America and then the French Republic, countries that differed from all that had existed before, two worldviews — two realities — split from one. The French

Revolution was a horror to people like Burke, but many Enlightenment thinkers were inspired by it. Jefferson was disturbed by the atrocities of the Terror, but he was steadfast in his support for revolution in France and elsewhere, as when he wrote in 1795: "This ball of liberty, I believe most piously, is now so well in motion that it will roll round the globe, at least the enlightened part of it, for light & liberty go together."[17]

The split between people living within Enlightenment and Counter-Enlightenment worldviews has persisted ever since, causing conflict, and sometimes violence, even as it has gone unrecognized. As I'll show, it now threatens to rip our democracy in two.

I'll also show how we may be able to heal the division.

But first, we must understand it.

What Is a Nation?

F ounded on social contracts rather than ethnicity or history, the United States and the French Republic were the first instances of what we now call the civic nation.

The French historian Ernest Renan saw the civic nation as the only legitimate nation. In an 1882 speech at the Sorbonne, Renan defined a nation as a voluntary association, based primarily on shared ideas and desires, and only secondarily on a shared history — a history that may well be based on fiction, and a necessary forgetting of past conflicts. He denied race and a race-based culture as bases for nationality:

> The truth is that there is no pure race and that to make politics depend upon ethnographic analysis is to surrender it to a chimera...

> A nation's existence is... a daily plebiscite, just as an individual's existence is a perpetual affirmation of life. That, I know full well, is less metaphysical than divine right and less brutal than so-called historical right... We have driven metaphysical and theological abstractions out of politics. What then remains? Man, with his desires and his needs.[18]

Renan could be confident in his Enlightenment-based analysis because of the examples set by the civic nations of America and France.

But meanwhile the Counter-Enlightenment was generating counter-examples: the first "nation-states." These were explicitly intended to be based on race and culture, not contracts. They were ethnic nations, not civic ones.

Two of the first nation-states were the German Empire (1871) and the Kingdom of Italy (1861). Each was conceived as the homeland of a quasi-historical ethnic tribe.

Germany originated in the *Volkisch* movement, named for the *Volk,* a supposed ancient, noble German race. German philosophers and artists provided a supporting ethos of "blood and soil" — this unique race sprung from this unique land — and the *geist,* or spirit, of the nation. Such themes were developed in the works of Hamann, Goethe, Schiller, Hegel, Wagner, and other figures of German Romanticism and the pre-Romantic *Sturm und Drang* movement.

Wagner's life mission was to express the full history of the German *geist* by bringing together music, poetry, scenery, and performance in a "total work of art," or *gesamtkunstwerk.* His magnum opus, *The Ring of the Nibelung,* opens with an image of the original *volk* in a state of innocent joy: the laughing Rhine maidens. They guard the *Rheingold* — the nation's essential wealth and power. The lecherous, cunning dwarf (*nibelung*) Alberich comes upon them, and they at first make fun of his advances. But Alberich tricks them into revealing the secret to claiming the gold: renouncing love. As he is about to grab his prize, Alberich sings:

> I shall inherit the world for myself through you
> I may not get love by force,
> but enforce covetousness with cunning
>
> *terrifyingly loud*
>
> Just carry on mocking!
> Unto your gold, the Nibelung is nigh![19]

In the first minutes of this massive work, Wagner portrays the corruption of the traditional German nation, a land of magic, nobility, and love. Alberich embodies greed, duplicity, and soullessness: the modern, post-Enlightenment world.

Not at all incidentally, Alberich is not only a dwarf, a common character in old German and Norse mythology. The audience for the 1876 Bayreuth premiere would have recognized him as a stereotypical Jew. Wagner was both a musical genius and a vicious anti-Semite. In an 1850 essay called "Judaism in Music," he wrote:

> We have no need to first substantiate the be-Jewing of modern art; it springs to the eye, and thrusts upon the senses, of itself... If emancipation from the yoke of Judaism appears to us the greatest of necessities, we must hold it weighty above all to prove our forces for this war of liberation. Now we shall never win these forces from an abstract definition of that phenomenon per se, but only from an accurate acquaintance with the nature of that involuntary feeling of ours which utters itself as an instinctive repugnance against the Jew's prime essence...
>
> The Jew... in ordinary life strikes us primarily by his outward appearance, which, no matter to what European nationality we belong, has something disagreeably foreign to that nationality: instinctively we wish to have nothing in common with a man who looks like that.[20]

Within the Enlightenment worldview, anti-Semitism is not only hateful, but, like other forms of bigotry, makes no sense: Why would anyone even care whether another person is Jewish, or a member of any other group, beyond possibly finding it interesting?

But to an ethnic nationalist like Wagner, the problem started with Jews' statelessness. They were not *of* the nation, nor of any nation: no matter where they might go, they were inherently foreign. This made them not only objects of fear and suspicion, but ready receptacles for all the dark elements to be cast out of one's own national character. It is Alberich who is greedy, aggressive, and repulsive. The German Rhine maidens are pure, like the gold they protect.

Wagner's *gesamtkunstwerk,* which is composed of some of history's most beautiful art and its ugliest prejudices, is a total expression not only of his German nationalism, but of the Counter-Enlightenment itself, both then and now.

In Italy, the *volk* were the ethnic Italians, who also had somewhat mythical origins. Many had been trapped in the *irredenta*, the "unredeemed" territories under foreign domination. They were redeemed by the *Risorgimento* ("Resurgence"), which created the Kingdom of Italy in 1861.

An ethnic nationalist resurgence occurred in France as well, after it had been transformed so radically into a civic nation. France became an empire again under Napoleon, then a monarchy in the Bourbon Restoration of 1815, went through a second civic revolution in 1848, and then was plagued by episodes of reinvigorated ethnic intolerance, including the anti-Semitism of the Dreyfus Affair (1894-1906), and the sympathy for Nazism among members of the French nationalist right from the 1930s through the Occupation — during which, the puppet Vichy regime replaced France's civic nationalist motto of "Liberty, Equality, and Fraternity" with the ethnic nationalist "Work, Family, Fatherland."

In America, too, it turned out that ethnic nationalism had not been declared out of existence. For a start, "all men are created equal" excluded women, Africans, and Natives. Women would not get the vote until 1920, the Constitution counted a slave as three-fifths of a person, and Enlightenment values did little to stop the displacement and killing of Native Americans.

The civic nation's map was not its territory. America's territory had been settled by people who were ethnically English, Scots, Dutch, German, Swedish, and Finnish. They included religious Pilgrims, monarchists, and cultural traditionalists, who found themselves in a nation that from now on would be ruled by rationalists. Some left for Canada, where they would be known as United Empire Loyalists.

Even those who remained and swore loyalty to the civic nation held onto ethnic nationalist assumptions. Jefferson himself embodied some of the tensions built into the new country's design.

Jefferson the Enlightenment rationalist thought he could simply edit the miracles out of the Bible and turn it into a work of moral philosophy.[21] But the culture of Jefferson's native South was based on traditional, rural, and aristocratic Counter-Enlightenment values, which Jefferson subscribed to himself to one degree and another, especially in his strong preference for a rural society. And while he was one of our most powerfully eloquent advocates for equality, and at least partially acknowledged his own hypocrisy in the matter, he owned slaves throughout his life.

The Lewis and Clark Expedition (1804-06) carried both the Enlightenment and the Counter-Enlightenment westward. Its objectives (set by then-President Jefferson) were to find routes for commerce, establish territorial claims before the British and other European competitors could, and to conduct research in botany, zoology, and geography.

The commercial and scientific parts of the mission were firmly within the Enlightenment mode. The Counter-Enlightenment came along in the forms of preparing the way for further displacement of Native Americans, evangelizing by Christian pastors and missionaries, and the establishment of more slave states along with free ones.

As the young country grew, so too would the tension between the two worldviews.

The Battle Between & Within

W hile people of the Counter-Enlightenment worldview could often be found pursuing ethnocentric conquest and exploitation, some were strong advocates for tolerance and compassion, with religious Abolitionists at the forefront. Christians had inherited a long, though often interrupted, tradition of opposition to slavery from St. Gregory of Nyssa (335-395 CE), who said, "Not all the universe would constitute an adequate payment for the soul of a mortal."[22] Although the Bible depicts slavery as a normal feature of society, the New Testament is a primary source for Western concepts of equality, which were developed by later Christian thinkers such as Martin Luther, and were advanced by Puritans and Quakers in the American colonies.

Conversely, Enlightenment reason was often deployed to provide pseudoscientific or legalistic justifications for ethnocentrism, including slavery and even genocide. President Andrew Jackson (in office 1829-37) based his case for expelling Native Americans on "progress," as well as on the prospect of an even worse fate if they remained in their ancestral lands. In his First Annual Message to Congress in 1829, Jackson said:

> Humanity has often wept over the fate of the aborigines of this country, and Philanthropy has been long busily employed in devising means to avert it, but its progress has never for a moment been arrested, and one by one have many powerful tribes disappeared from the earth. To follow to the tomb the last of his race and to tread on the graves of extinct nations excite melancholy reflections. But true philanthropy reconciles the mind to these vicissitudes as it does to the extinction of one generation to make room for another. In the monuments and fortresses of an unknown people, spread over the extensive regions of the West, we behold the memorials of a once

powerful race, which was exterminated or has disappeared to make room for the existing savage tribes. Nor is there anything in this which, upon a comprehensive view of the general interests of the human race, is to be regretted. Philanthropy could not wish to see this continent restored to the conditions in which it was found by our forefathers. What good man would prefer a country covered with forests and ranged by a few thousand savages to our extensive Republic, studded with cities, towns, and prosperous farms, embellished with all the improvements which art can devise or industry execute, occupied by more than 12,000,000 happy people, and filled with all the blessings of liberty, civilization, and religion?[23]

Jackson is a forefather of the "America First" form of patriotism and foreign policy, which has re-appeared in various versions ever since. Trump adviser Steve Bannon, an avowed and proud ethnonationalist, recommended the portrait of Jackson that currently hangs in the Oval Office.

Following Jackson's presidency, the tension between civic and ethnic nationalism only increased. In 1861, it exploded.

The Civil War would be fought in the first place over slavery, as the Confederates themselves declared, but it was also a revolt of the Counter-Enlightenment against the Enlightenment.[24] Southern mythologists still eulogize it as "The Lost Cause," eliding the Old South's vicious economics. It's a Wagnerian recasting of history: The Old South, bucolic, innocent, and noble, valiantly resisting the industrial, greedy, and corrupt Yankees.

Six hundred and twenty thousand Americans died, fighting for two nations.

With the Confederacy's defeat in 1865, the Enlightenment vision of America finally appeared to have been made real, and triumphant. But the Counter-Enlightenment resistance never stopped fighting that vision. After assassinating the Great Emancipator Abraham Lincoln, John Wilkes Booth shouted "Sic semper tyrannis!" ("Thus always to tyrants!") States of the former Confederacy immediately began seeking ways to sabotage the Northern victory, such as through Black Codes restricting the rights of African Americans. Lincoln's successor as President, Andrew Johnson, was a slave-owner until 1863, believed that the decision to free slaves should be made by states, and vetoed the Civil Rights Act of 1866, which guaranteed important rights, although not the right to vote, for African Americans (Republicans in Congress then passed it over Johnson's veto).

The American Counter-Enlightenment continued to the present day, as did the conflict between the two worldviews — often, as with Jefferson and with Rousseau, within our own minds.

A Counter-Enlightenment history of the United States would include these events, movements, and philosophies:

- The political concept, favored by Johnson, of states' rights. Often, this was just a cover for the defense of slavery, but it also was an example of the Counter-Enlightenment preference for the local and specific over the global and systematic. The pairing of hateful motives with defensible ones persists to the present, for example in the hostility to "globalists." This antipathy is sometimes localist, sometimes anti-Semitic, and sometimes both.
- The religious Great Awakenings, starting from the 1730s and extending to the present-day evangelical movement.
- The Transcendentalism of Emerson, Thoreau, and others, the roots of which were in Christianity, Hinduism, Swedenborgian Theosophism, Romanticism, and Kantian idealism.
- Exploitation of Chinese laborers, and ethnic restrictions on immigration and citizenship such as the Chinese Exclusion Act of 1882.
- Post-Civil War backlash against civil rights, throughout Reconstruction, Jim Crow, and to the present.
- Enforced cultural assimilation of Native Americans.[25]
- Anti-Catholicism and anti-Semitism.
- The post-World War I resurgence of the Ku Klux Klan, fueled in large part by D.W. Griffiths' movie *The Birth of a Nation*.[26]
- Eugenics theory and policies based on it.
- The 1925 Scopes "Monkey" trial over the teaching of evolution in Tennessee, where that was illegal.
- The internment of Japanese-Americans during World War II.
- The 1960s counterculture, which encompassed revivals of Transcendentalism, Symbolism, Da Da, the occult, mythology, and other

non-rationalist pursuits of the past, as well a reverence for indigenous people — who were often romanticized as Rousseauian noble savages — and a preference for ethnic musical styles like folk, blues, and, of course, soul, named for exactly what modern culture seemed to be missing.

- The backlash to the counterculture, based on traditional values and/or resistance to civil rights.
- The rise of the Tea Party, which along with its libertarianism included strong currents of ethnonationalism and xenophobia.
- Trumpism.

Across the world, a similar resistance, Counter-Enlightenment vs. Enlightenment, was enacted over the same timeline.

Charles Darwin's theory of natural selection, published in his *On the Origin of Species* in 1859, was the most direct assault yet by science against religion, removing God from natural history. In 1882, philosopher Friedrich Nietzsche declared that following the Enlightenment and discoveries such as Darwin's, "God is dead."[27]

The science-driven Industrial Revolution yielded unprecedented growth and a new and prosperous social class, the bourgeoisie, who created wealth instead of inheriting it. But its slums and factories generated unprecedented misery. William Blake expressed his horror at it all in the Preface to his *Milton: A Poem in Two Books* (1810), breaking from prose into poetry:

> …There is a Class of Men whose whole delight is in
> Destroying. We do not want either Greek or Roman Models if
> we are but just & true to our own Imaginations, those Worlds
> of Eternity in which we shall live for ever, in Jesus Our Lord.

> *And did those feet in ancient time*
> *Walk upon England's mountains green,*
> *And was the holy Lamb of God*
> *On England's pleasant pastures seen.*

> *And did the Countenance Divine*
> *Shine forth upon our clouded hills?*
> *And was Jerusalem builded here*
> *Among these dark Satanic Mills?*

Bring me my Bow of burning gold:
Bring me my Arrows of desire:
Bring me my Spear: O clouds unfold!
Bring me my Chariot of fire:

I will not cease from Mental Fight,
Nor shall my Sword sleep in my hand,
Till we have built Jerusalem,
In England's green & pleasant Land.[28]

The suffering that fueled those "dark, satanic mills" provoked both Counter-Enlightenment responses, like Blake's, and others rooted in the Enlightenment. Karl Marx witnessed similar sights while living in London, in poverty, from 1849 until his death in 1883. While Blake's answer was poetic witness, Marx's was an Enlightenment-based, rationalist, though fundamentally mistaken solution to the problem of inequality.

Marx had his Counter-Enlightenment aspects, too, though. His belief that human nature is inherently good in the absence of private property evoked not only Wagnerian mythology but the Garden of Eden, and his belief that revolution could heal the world was a form of millenarianism. As Blake may have been as well, Marx was also quite an anti-Semite, as can be seen in his 1843 essay "On the Jewish Question."[29]

While science was making industry much more productive, it had done the same with war.

After the French Revolution triggered attacks on France by nations of the old order, Napoleon mobilized the entire French population, announcing that he was willing to accept nearly limitless casualties. He was given the opportunity. Thanks to modern artillery — and pre-modern medicine — millions of Europeans died.

Still, the Napoleonic Wars were a mere foreshadowing of the mechanized horrors of World War I battlefields, where plumed helmets and swords met machine guns and poison gas.

Led by Britain and France, the exhausted victors of the Great War obliviously and clumsily drew new civic nations on the ethnic nationalist territory of the Middle East, yielding the conflict that has raged there ever since.[30] The United

States then retreated from Woodrow Wilson's Enlightenment vision of the League of Nations into America First isolationism.

Enlightenment political values found new expression through Progressivism, which reached a peak in America with the enactment of Franklin Delano Roosevelt's New Deal. But conservatism surged in response, championed by economists Ludwig von Mises, F.A. Hayek, and their descendants in the Chicago School. Where many Progressives looked to socialism for inspiration, Hayek saw it as *The Road to Serfdom:*

> We have progressively abandoned that freedom in economic
> affairs without which personal and political freedom has never
> existed in the past. Although we had been warned by some of
> the greatest political thinkers of the nineteenth century, by
> Tocqueville and Lord Acton, that socialism means slavery, we
> have steadily moved in the direction of socialism...[31]

Although the highly rational Hayek frequently thought in the Enlightenment mode, central to his economic philosophy was the Counter-Enlightenment argument — drawing on Adam Smith's concept of the "invisible hand" — that a nation's economy should not be designed. Hayek argued that it will work better, and avoid harms to liberty, if the economy emerges from the spontaneous actions of individuals:

> During the whole of this modern period of European history
> the general direction of social development was one of freeing
> the individual from the ties which had bound him to the
> customary or prescribed ways in the pursuit of his ordinary
> activities... The subsequent elaboration of a consistent
> argument in favor of economic freedom was the outcome of a
> free growth of economic activity which had been the
> undesigned and unforeseen by-product of political freedom.[32]

The coming of the Second World War saw the Counter-Enlightenment gone mad: the ultra-*Volkisch* Nazis marching behind Roman swastikas, Mussolini's black-shirted *Fascisti*, and the Empire of Japan, whose militarism had roots in the Sonnō jōi movement of resistance to "barbarian" invaders like the Americans and the British. Taken to the furthest extreme, Counter-Enlightenment

Romanticism and ethnonationalism birthed the Holocaust, along with other atrocities such as the Nanjing Massacre.

Meanwhile the Soviet Union, and the other communist dictatorships that followed its lead, represented the equally terrible alternative of the Enlightenment gone mad. Marxist-Leninism was founded on Marx's tragically wrong "science" of history, implemented with the intolerance for "error" of the French Revolution's Jacobins. Marx believed that history was a rational and materialistic process of economic class conflict, between proletarians and capitalists. But reality refused to fit theory. The forced transmogrification of real Russian peasants into theoretical Soviet proletarians produced tens of millions of deaths, along with the imprisonment, torture, and murder of uncounted political dissidents. Mao Zedong would visit a similar fate on his country's people, as would Cambodia's Pol Pot, among others who believed history was scientific.

As the Polish poet, writer, and one-time diplomat Czeslaw Milosz wrote in the bitterly satirical "Child of Europe" (1946):

> He who has power, has it by historical logic.
> Respectfully bow to that logic...
>
> Learn to predict a fire with unerring precision
> Then burn the house down to fulfill the prediction.[33]

"The Center Cannot Hold"

B oth fascists and communists were so grievously wrong because of what was excluded from their extreme Counter-Enlightenment and Enlightenment worldviews: reason from one, soul from the other. Fascism and communism proved to be two sides of the same totalitarian coin: the Final Solution — ethnic purity — vs. the final explanation — scientific accuracy.

Sigmund Freud bridged the two worldviews, while resisting their extremes. In many ways, Freud was an exemplary Enlightenment rationalist, and his legacy has tended to live among the Enlightenment's heirs, though not without dispute of some of his hypotheses, notably those about women and homosexuality.

But as rational as he was, Freud's explorations of the psyche revealed to him its irrational depths. To describe them, he resorted not to science but to mythology. Mythological symbols and characters — Eros, Oedipus, Elektra, and the rest — are found throughout Freud's writings.

Freud saw that human nature would refuse to cooperate with management. His *Civilization and Its Discontents*, published in 1930, was based on both his own research and the awful lessons of World War I. Marx had thought that private property was the source of humans' cruelty to each other; Freud thought Marx was naïve:

> I have no doubt… that a real change in people's relations to property will be of more help here than any ethical commandment; yet the recognition of this fact among socialists has been obscured and made impracticable by a new idealistic misreading of human nature.[34]

Looking to the future, Freud was decidedly *non*-idealistic. He foresaw a technology-enabled struggle between humanity's opposing urges towards life and death:

> The fateful question for the human race seems to be whether, and to what extent, the development of its civilization will manage to overcome the disturbance of communal life caused by the human drive for aggression and self-destruction... Human beings have made such strides in controlling the forces of nature that, with the help of these forces, they will have no difficulty in exterminating one another, down to the last man. They know this, and it is this knowledge that accounts for much of their present disquiet, unhappiness and anxiety. And now it is to be expected that the other of the two 'heavenly powers', immortal Eros, will try to assert himself in the struggle with his equally immortal adversary. But who can foresee the outcome?[35]

Not only through his work but through his life as a Jewish Austrian, Freud saw all too clearly that both reason and unreason could spawn nightmares.

So did others. Following the senseless slaughter of World War I, sense-making itself was in question. It appeared that no matter what system humanity comes up with, "things fall apart; the center cannot hold," as W.B. Yeats wrote in 1919, in "The Second Coming."

Each new discovery of the modern world seemed to cause a new fall from grace, in endless recapitulations of Genesis. "After such knowledge, what forgiveness?" asked T.S. Eliot in "Gerontion" (1920).

In his 1917 lecture "Science as a Vocation," sociologist Max Weber spoke of a less violent but still painful form of loss: the removal of mystery and magic from the modern world:

> The fate of our times is characterized by rationalization and intellectualization and, above all, by the disenchantment of the world. Precisely the ultimate and most sublime values have retreated from public life either into the transcendental realm of mystic life or into the brotherliness of direct and personal human relations. It is no accident that our greatest art is intimate and not monumental.[36]

A series of artistic movements would explode assumptions about order and reason: these included fauvism, cubism, jazz, surrealism, Dadaism, expressionism, aleatoric (random) composition, and the Theatre of the Absurd.

Philosophy saw its core assumptions about reason challenged, via movements such as logical positivism, phenomenology, critical theory, existentialism, and poststructuralism. Many philosophers concluded the gap between language and reality was unbridgeable. In his *Philosophical Investigations* (published posthumously in 1953), Ludwig Wittgenstein said, "If a lion could talk, we would not be able to understand him." Wittgenstein meant that a lion's worldview would be too different from ours for the lion's comments to make any sense to us. Postmodern philosophers saw language as a tool not for describing an objective reality, but for constructing reality and asserting power over it. Jacques Derrida's deconstruction method was used to expose how that worked.

Ironically, while deconstruction was associated with leftist French theoreticians like Derrida and Michel Foucault, it was put into practice by conservative American politicians. The latter realized that deconstruction was not only a theory for critiquing society, but a set of instructions for reshaping it, by subverting Enlightenment assumptions about governing. A senior official in the George W. Bush administration boasted about that to Ron Suskind of The New York Times:

> The aide said that guys like me were "in what we call the reality-based community," which he defined as people who "believe that solutions emerge from your judicious study of discernible reality." I nodded and murmured something about enlightenment principles and empiricism. He cut me off. "That's not the way the world really works anymore," he continued. "We're an empire now, and when we act, we create our own reality. And while you're studying that reality — judiciously, as you will — we'll act again, creating other new realities, which you can study too, and that's how things will sort out. We're history's actors ... and you, all of you, will be left to just study what we do."[37]

"Print the Legend"

S cience had seemed to promise a much more accurate depiction of reality. But through its disruptions, science had called reality itself into question. And increasingly, science was used to create reality, through the industrialization of communication. This took the forms of mass-scale news, entertainment, marketing, and the merger of those three, propaganda. Delivered more and more via images and sound instead of words, all would become powerful Counter-Enlightenment influences on culture.

Although the most dramatic impacts have been seen relatively recently, the use of media to shape perception dates to when the medium was a clay tablet. Here's an example of a "praise poem" from ancient Sumer, this one for Ur-Namma, who ruled from 2112-2095 BCE:

> Under Ur-Namma, king of Urim, for whom a favorable destiny
> was determined, the roads have been made passable. An opens
> his holy mouth, and because of me rain is produced. He directs
> it downward into the earth, and abundance is brought for me.
> Enlil treats me kindly, ... Enki treats me kindly, bestowing
> early floods, grain and dappled barley. Nintud formed me; I am
> peerless... I am the king of the Land... Under my rule the
> cattle-pens and sheepfolds are extended wide. Utu endowed me
> with eloquence (?); my judgments create concord in Sumer and
> Akkad. Ningubalag has given me strength. In the whole extent
> of heaven and earth, no one can escape from a battle with me.[38]

Change the details and one could expect to hear much the same thing coming from a TV today.

It took many centuries for media technology to progress from clay to parchment. Then, around 1439, there was a sudden leap forward, with the invention of the movable type printing press by Johannes Gutenberg (in China, movable type may have been introduced roughly 500 years earlier).

Among the most significant productions of Gutenberg's press were affordable Bibles in the vernacular, which allowed people to study scripture for themselves, and thus prepared the way for the Protestant Reformation, which in turn would be a source of the Enlightenment. Martin Luther's Ninety-Five Theses (1517) also owed their impact to the press: they would hardly have had the same effect if they only had been nailed to a church door in Wittenberg.

In response to the challenge from Protestants, the Catholic Church set up its own propaganda effort, which in 1622 would take the form of the Sacred Congregation for Propagation of the Faith, or *Propaganda Fide.*

The deployment of propaganda and other forms of mass communication leapt another order of magnitude with the Industrial Revolution. Industrialization would yield, in rough order: fast publishing at massive scale, visual reproduction by photography and later cinematography, sound reproduction by phonograph, fast distribution by railroad, instantaneous distribution by telegraph, instantaneous sound transmission by telephone and radio, and instantaneous visual transmission by television. Later, the Information Age would bring instantaneous, interactive communication using all channels: words, images, sounds, and haptics (sensations).

By the early 20th century, entertainment, marketing, news, and propaganda had gained a power to shape culture that rivaled any religion or philosophy.

Hollywood and the record business offered celebrities to replace the nobles and gods that rationalism had taken from us. Advertising offered consumer products to feed our instinctive needs, such as for status, power, and sexual success. The "yellow press" offered unending novelty and sensation, and made magnates of William Randolph Hearst and Joseph Pulitzer.[39]

"Women are not in love with me but with the picture of me they see on the screen. I am merely the canvas upon which the women paint their dreams," said Rudolf Valentino, the first screen idol.[40] Valentino's image was so powerful that following his sudden death at age 31 in 1926, some fans reportedly attempted suicide. He was the prototype for superstars to come, such as Sinatra, Elvis, The Beatles, Michael Jackson, and Beyoncé.

Marketers used the power of images, sounds, and emotion to boost the sales of nonessential products, by making those products *feel* essential. Public relations pioneer Edward Bernays was a direct descendant of Freud — like the industry he helped create. A resounding early success was Bernays' "Torches of Freedom" campaign on behalf of the American Tobacco Company. This linked cigarette smoking with women's emancipation — the "torches" were cigarettes. A Torches of Freedom march in the 1929 New York Easter Sunday parade became a global news story, women's smoking lost its previous social stigma, and sales skyrocketed.

World War I had seen the adoption of propaganda as a weapon on an unprecedented scale. It was mastered thereafter by the Nazis and other authoritarians of the right and left. Spectacle, lights, sound, and costumes undoubtedly recruited Nazis more effectively than ideology alone ever could: hence the centrality of Goebbels' Ministry of Propaganda, the Nuremberg rallies, and Leni Riefenstahl's *Triumph of the Will*.

Less overt forms of influence used the same kinds of media resources. The effects were often indirect, or even accidental, though hardly less powerful.

Among countless examples that could be cited: the archetype of the cowboy, as presented in 19th century novels, news stories, paintings, road shows, and the movies, radio serials, and TV programs that followed. Few symbols are as central to American culture. The cowboy embodies courage, character, boundless freedom, and a Romantic, Counter-Enlightenment flight from civilization — a civilization represented by another archetype, the fancy-pants, Eastern or (worse) European city slicker.

The cowboy, as known by most of the world, was largely a fiction. His image and ethos come to us through media, by way of James Fenimore Cooper, Frederic Remington, Buffalo Bill, John Ford and John Wayne, the Marlboro Man, Clint Eastwood, and Ronald Reagan, among others.

Speaking of the Marlboro Man, it's hard to imagine now, but that character transformed Marlboro cigarettes from a ladies' brand to one for men, strictly through the power of the commercialized form of symbolism known as branding. Ad agency head Leo Burnett explained in a 1972 documentary:

> "Here's where I went... 'Some people think that filtered cigarettes are sissy.' I said, 'What's the most masculine symbol you can think of?' And right off the top of his head one of these writers spoke up and said a cowboy. And I said, 'That's for sure.'"[41]

Ronald Reagan began his career playing cowboys and other heroes; he ended it as President of the United States and a hero to many millions. Whether deliberately or not, Reagan himself sometimes seemed to lose track of the distinction between fiction and real life. His White House staff grew used to it. When challenged on the veracity of a story of military heroism Reagan had told many times, spokesman Larry Speakes jokingly quoted a Southern saying: "If you tell the same story five times, it's true."[42] That recalled the line spoken by a reporter near the ending of the iconic Ford/Wayne western *The Man Who Shot Liberty Valance:* "This is the West, sir. When the legend becomes fact, print the legend."[43]

Now, as anyone who has spent time in the American west can tell you, there are real cowboys, who match the fictional archetype. The thing is, the archetype was the model for them, instead of the other way around.

Because of the cowboy's individualism, he has come to be associated with conservatism. I don't want to suggest, though, that media archetypes are only at work on the right. All of us, at least to some degree, pattern our personalities on fictional characters, along with real people in our lives — who themselves can hardly have avoided influence by fictional characters.[44]

Before Reagan rode to the White House, John F. Kennedy had come to embody a different, but equally influential, fictional archetype: the wounded Fisher King, the keeper of the Holy Grail, which had held Christ's blood. The Fisher King has also taken many other forms, including Siegfried (namesake of one of the four acts of Wagner's *Ring*), Parsifal, King Arthur, Roy Hobbs in Bernard Malamud's 1952 novel *The Natural,* the title character of the 1991 Terry Gilliam/Robin Williams movie, and Bran Stark in the TV series *Game of Thrones.* Bran is named after Bran Fendigaid ("The Blessed"), said to have been given the Grail by Joseph of Arimathea and to have taken it to the British Isles.[45]

Kennedy's TV-friendly good looks and winning personality helped make him a celebrity as well as a politician. One week after his assassination on Nov.

22, 1963, he became something more. Jackie Kennedy asked Theodore White, a highly sympathetic reporter, to come to the family compound in Hyannis Port, Massachusetts. There she and White wrote the myth of a new Camelot, borrowing from the recent hit Broadway musical of that name: "Don't let it be forgot, that once there was a spot, for one brief, shining moment that was known as Camelot."

White told the story in a special edition of Life magazine.[46] And thus the president of an Enlightenment democracy, known to insiders more for calculating realism than romantic idealism, was reborn as a symbolic Fisher King, through the Counter-Enlightenment power of image, emotion, myth — and media.[47]

His Majesty the Baby

The news, entertainment, and marketing industries depend for their survival on gaining, holding, and monetizing our attention. In so doing, they also must lavish *their* attention upon us. They must learn what we want.

The more that what people want is catered to, the more likely it is that they will be infantilized.

The causes of narcissism are complex and not fully understood. But Freud's insight about the role of anxious, hyper-attentive parents has stood up:

> If we look at the attitude of affectionate parents towards their children, we have to recognize that it is a revival and reproduction of their own narcissism, which they have long since abandoned.... They are under a compulsion to ascribe every perfection to the child—which sober observation would find no occasion to do—and to conceal and forget all his shortcomings... The child shall have a better time than his parents; he shall not be subject to the necessities which they have recognized as paramount in life. Illness, death, renunciation of enjoyment, restrictions on his own will, shall not touch him; the laws of nature and of society shall be abrogated in his favour; he shall once more really be the centre and core of creation — 'His Majesty the Baby', as we once fancied ourselves.[48]

All of us in the modern, developed world receive anxious, hyper-attentive parenting, for our whole lives, through media.

That's because there's so much money to be made in giving us what we want. Since the Industrial Revolution, and especially since World War II, the developed world has experienced prosperity that is orders of magnitude beyond all previous economic history. We can see it in the suddenly vertical graph of global gross domestic product (GDP) since the year 1 CE. It's more than just growth; it's a change of state:

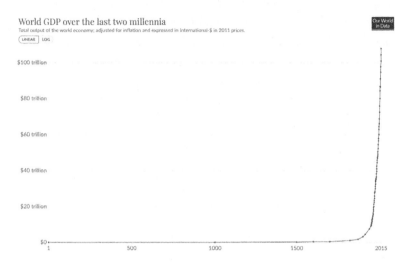

World GDP over the last two millennia
Total output of the world economy; adjusted for inflation and expressed in international-$ in 2011 prices.

Source: Our World in Data website, Oxford Martin School, University of Oxford[49]

Not only did the amount of production explode, the kind of production was transformed: from meeting our needs to meeting our desires. Consumption now makes up about 70 percent of GDP.[50]

As a result, recent history is different from any our ancestors could have imagined. The more prosperous slices of the Baby Boom generation and its descendants have been indulged beyond the dreams of the royalty of ages past. In particular, starting in the 1950s, significant industries cared, for the first time, about what children and adolescents wanted. News, entertainment, marketing, and then politics began to revolve around young people.

The new power of youth led to cultural change such as never had been seen before.

Much of that change was positive, especially when it overturned old prejudices, or disrupted the often-stifling conformity of the postwar mainstream, as captured in the stereotype of the "organization man" (named for William H. Whyte's 1956 book).

But all that new, commercialized attention directed at youth may have had less salutary effects as well, as might be expected with advertising slogans standing in for the crib-side cooing of Mom and Dad.

Because there are so many variables involved, we should be cautious in making assertions about trends in psychology and culture, but there appears to have been a dramatic rise in the incidence of narcissism in the postwar West. For example, the percentage of US adolescents who agreed with the statement "I am an important person" rose from 12 percent in 1963 to as high as 80 percent in 1992.[51] A measure of grandiose narcissism as self-reported among US college students rose 30 percent between 1979 and 2006.[52]

Two pop songs with the same name expressed two aspects of the new culture: "Give the People What They Want" by the O'Jays (1975) and by the Kinks (1981).

The O'Jays sang about social justice:

> Well, it's about time for things to get better
> We want the truth, the truth and no more lies
> We want freedom, justice and equality
> I want it for you and I want it for me…
>
> Got to give the people
> Give the people what they want.[53]

But the Kinks sang about narcissistic consumerism:

> Give the people what they want
> You gotta give the people what they want
> The more they get, the more they need
> And every time they get harder and harder to please.[54]

In highlighting the rise of narcissism, I'm aware that throughout history, every generation has complained about the ones that have come after it, going back at least to Aristotle in the 4th century BCE:

> All their mistakes are in the direction of doing things
> excessively and vehemently. They disobey Chilon's precept by
> overdoing everything, they love too much and hate too much,
> and the same thing with everything else. They think they know

everything, and are always quite sure about it; this, in fact, is why they overdo everything.[55]

Further, let me stipulate again that young people of the sixties and beyond have made many important and valuable contributions to society, including, not least, great songs like my examples here.

But I'm actually most concerned about my own generation and our influence as parents — I came along at the tail end of the Baby Boom. It's hard, not just for me but for many of my peers, not to feel that with the hyperbolic postwar growth in prosperity, something changed in our character, in a way that previously wouldn't have been possible, because such conditions had never existed before. That feeling amplifies our reverence and nostalgia for the Greatest Generation, who — when *they* were young — risked everything to save the world for us and handed us a legacy of such freedom and opportunity. Among those heroes were civil rights leaders who suffered beatings, torture, and murder, so that the legacy could be shared more fairly.

By contrast, subsequent generations seem to have become more and more obsessed with their own needs. Turning inward can be healthy, psychologically and spiritually. But those who are able to do so have, relative to previous generations, luxurious amounts of time and money. They support a self-realization industry that has grown up around them, and which has saturated popular culture as well. Many times per day, from movies, TV shows, songs, books, articles, ads, and each other, we hear, "you're special," "you deserve this," "trust your heart," "go with your gut," "follow your dreams," and similar messages. Such free-floating slogans seem to be at least as influential as whatever ethical lessons we've retained from philosophy, religion, literature, or history.

For people on the left, it's easy to spot signs of narcissism on the right, which is, after all, the side that celebrates individualism. It's all the easier to point to supporters of Trump. Many psychologists and psychiatrists have broken with their usual professional reticence to warn that Trump is severely narcissistic, sociopathic, or both.[56] It's tempting to apply the same diagnosis to people who, say, demand the right to risk spreading the coronavirus in the name of "freedom."

But liberals can be self-obsessed in their own ways. Even social activism sometimes has narcissistic characteristics, with the activist somehow ending up at the center of the drama. Of course, when people in power won't listen, you may have little choice but to demand change, like the American Revolutionaries did, and like activists have done ever since. Saul Alinsky, a pioneer of community organizing who influenced Cesar Chavez and a young Barack Obama, wrote a guidebook, *Rules for Radicals,* for turning an unresponsive system against itself so as to force it to recognize your demands.

But Alinsky's radicalism was based on the assumption that democracy didn't work for those who lacked power or money. That certainly was true for people who were denied jobs, equal pay, their vote, or even their basic safety. But Obama was one who ended up abandoning Alinsky's approach, when he came to believe that democracy, whatever its flaws, was working. Once outsiders had won some access to power, they could do more good by operating within the system than by attacking it from without.

Uncompromising radicals run the risk of taking on the very intolerance they're fighting. If making radical demands becomes the default mode in every situation, radicalism becomes hard to distinguish from tyranny — intolerance when the situation is not intolerable, but negotiable.

For many of us, radicalism became not a last resort but a first, and a cultural norm. "Radical" became a default term of approbation, along with "subversive" and "disruptive" — how many arts and entertainment reviews have you read that contain terms like these used as synonyms for "good?" More than you could count, I'll bet. At a certain point radicalism becomes its opposite, convention.

These days there are still people who face threats to their basic rights. But even many who are relatively safe and comfortable, on the right and the left, habitually demand maximalist solutions to problems, and will go on the attack if they don't get them immediately. They don't just disagree with their opponents, they "loathe" or "despise" them. Willingness to compromise is often associated with weakness or corruption, while a performance of righteous fury enhances one's status. Such is daily life on Twitter, a perfect platform for both communication and narcissism.

The Map Begins to Tear

For nearly a century following the Civil War, the Enlightenment-based, civic nationalist map of America more or less covered the rough ethnic territory.

But in the late 1950s, the map began to tear. Following World War II, it had looked like American society was slowly becoming more inclusive, more or less peacefully. The default culture was no longer strictly White Anglo-Saxon Protestant. It was still white, but the definition of "white" was expanding. Catholics, Jews, Italians, Slavs, the Irish, and others were slowly promoted from their original, lowly social positions, which had been barely above the lowest, the one forcibly imposed on African Americans.

And African Americans, too, were making some progress. After witnessing the mistreatment of black soldiers returning from overseas, President Truman desegregated the armed forces in 1948. He expressed regret for the racist attitudes he himself had held most of his life, born as he was into a Confederate family in Missouri. In 1954, the Supreme Court ruled in Brown v. Board of Education that "separate but equal" segregation was unconstitutional. Congress passed incremental civil rights legislation in 1957 and 1960.

But as progress built on progress, it accelerated. The 1964 Civil Rights Act and the 1965 Voting Rights Act were decidedly non-incremental. The repair of obvious injustices was moving towards the establishment of actual equality. That meant economic and cultural disruption, at all levels of society.

At the beginning of the sixties, the *idea* of equality had broad popular support, at least outside the South. But as Rick Perlstein recounts in his essential history *Nixonland,* once the *reality* of equality started to take hold, resistance rose dramatically:

Two political scientists crunched the opinion poll numbers and identified 1958 as the key date at which both parties were judged equally Negro-friendly. After that, the two parties diverged. The trend had been plotted through contingent accidents of history: John F. Kennedy's decision to phone Coretta Scott King with words of support as her husband sat in jail in Atlanta on the eve of the 1960 election, sending troops to integrate the University of Mississippi in 1962, introducing a sweeping civil rights bill in response to the violence in Birmingham in 1963; and Nixon sending Barry Goldwater to campaign for him in the South in 1960, then the selection of Barry Goldwater as the next Republican nominee.[57]

The upheaval in politics was accompanied by turmoil in the culture. Early rock and roll looks so innocent now, in *American Bandstand* kinescopes or *Happy Days* reruns. But it's hard to overstate the shock mainstream America felt as it witnessed the mixing of black and white musical styles in what many called "the Devil's music." Elvis Presley, a brilliant white performer who "sang black," was allowed to appear on TV only if the camera stayed above his hips, to prevent impressionable young people seeing that he "danced black," too.

Formerly, political divisions had been based on economics: Republicans for capital, Democrats for labor. Now they formed over race and culture.

Before the sixties, the Democratic Party had dominated government for decades, in large part because of an unholy bargain with racists, which had locked in a Democratic majority in the "Solid South." But in 1964, the Democrats lost the South virtually overnight. After signing the Civil Rights Act, President Lyndon Johnson said to his then aide Bill Moyers, "I think we just delivered the South to the Republican Party for a long time to come."[58] After Johnson, no Democratic presidential nominee would win a majority of the white vote.

Until that moment, the Republicans had proudly seen themselves as the Party of Lincoln. But now they saw a path out of the political wilderness: they could adopt the suddenly homeless "Dixiecrats."

Hence the 1968 Nixon campaign's invention of the Southern Strategy. Republican consultant Lee Atwater described it with the starkest, ugliest frankness, anonymously at the time, in a 1981 interview:

You start out in 1954 by saying, "Nigger, nigger, nigger." By 1968 you can't say "nigger"—that hurts you, backfires. So you say stuff like, uh, forced busing, states' rights, and all that stuff, and you're getting so abstract. Now, you're talking about cutting taxes, and all these things you're talking about are totally economic things and a byproduct of them is, blacks get hurt worse than whites.... "We want to cut this," is much more abstract than even the busing thing, uh, and a hell of a lot more abstract than "Nigger, nigger."[59]

In addition to a core team of Madison Avenue ad executives, along with ex-*Mike Douglas Show* producer Roger Ailes, the Nixon campaign hired an "ethnic specialist," consultant Kevin Phillips. Phillips explained what that meant to reporter Joe McGinnis for the classic inside-the-campaign account, *The Selling of the President:*

"Essentially what I do is determine what blocs can be moved in what states by what approach," [Phillips] said. 'Group susceptibility,' I call it.

"For instance, in Wisconsin you have Germans and you have Scandinavians, and the two groups respond to very different things. First, we determine where the groups are and then we decide how to reach them. What radio station each listens to, and so forth. I started too late to do it properly this year, but by 'seventy-two I should have it broken down county by county across the whole country so we'll be able to zero in on a much more refined target."[60]

Following the campaign, Phillips would publish *The Emerging Republican Majority,* which accurately predicted the political realignment we live within now.[61]

That realignment began almost immediately. In one election cycle, the civic nationalist map of America was replaced by an ethnic nationalist one.

The first of the following two maps shows the state-level breakdown of the 1964 Electoral College results. The second one is from just four years later.

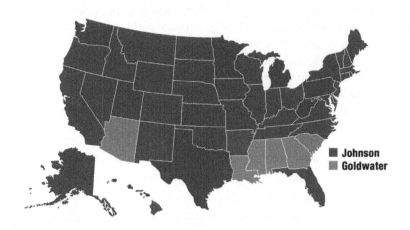

1964 Electoral College results. (Maps: the author/public domain.)

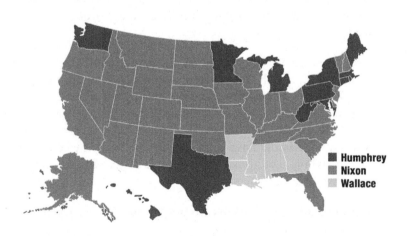

1968 Electoral College results.

In these two maps we can see not only the division of the country over ethnicity, but a rough indication of the roles of race and culture as ethnicity's components. Sometimes ethnicity is about culture; sometimes it's about race; and sometimes it's about both. In 1964, with the exception of Goldwater's home state of Arizona, Goldwater won only in the Deep South, the heart of former slave territory. It was still the place where racism was most culturally acceptable. Goldwater was very far to the right, both economically and culturally, but he could at least *claim* not to be a racist, and he needed to, for example by asserting that his opposition to the desegregation of restaurants was a libertarian defense of restaurant owners' private property rights.

In 1968, Nixon won all those newly red states by cloaking his race-based Southern Strategy in the cultural language of law and order and traditional values, as Atwater later described. Meanwhile the Deep South went for the explicitly racist George Wallace.

As hateful as Wallace was, at least you knew where he was coming from (he later changed his views and apologized). But ironically, as racism became less and less socially acceptable, it got harder to talk about it frankly. Some of the Democrats who suddenly switched to voting Republican were as racist as Wallace was. Some were racists but pretending not to be, maybe even to themselves. Some really didn't care all that much about race, but were alarmed by what they saw as threats to their culture, as the sixties upended respect for authority, religious observance, support for the military, traditional gender roles, the work ethic, and more. Racism was still common in explicit or implicit form throughout society, but it could hardly be mentioned without bringing to a halt any meaningful discussion of solutions.

Meanwhile, although ethnicity accounted for most of the sudden, radical change in the electoral map, economic factors had not disappeared. Many Democratic-turned-Republican voters would be hippies-turned-yuppies, whose motivations, now that they owned things, were probably economic. They were "socially liberal, but economically conservative."

Because of a mix of racial, cultural, and economic motivations, after the sixties there was an X-shaped movement across party lines. Many conservative Democrats became what would be called "Reagan Democrats" and then full-on Republicans.

Meanwhile, educated, socially liberal Republicans became "Rockefeller Republicans," so-named after the moderate New York Governor and then US Vice President Nelson Rockefeller. As the main body of the GOP moved further and further to the cultural right, rightists would call moderates RINOs, or

Republicans In Name Only. Some of the RINOs would end up calling themselves Democrats.

The Global Elite

For a while, the middle of the X — moderately liberal or conservative — looked like the place to be. In 1972, Democrat George McGovern had suffered a disastrous defeat after running far to the left of Nixon. Here's *that* map:

The Democratic Party has selected moderate nominees ever since, although not without challenges from the progressive left, including the strong ones by Bernie Sanders in 2016 and 2020.

The Republicans moved to the middle as well, at least officially, while continuing to rely on the Southern Strategy unofficially: Ronald Reagan launched his 1980 campaign in Philadelphia, MI, where three civil rights activists happened to have been murdered in 1964; the George H.W. Bush campaign, under the direction of Lee Atwater, ran the race-baiting Willie Horton TV ad, and allies of George W. Bush targeted John McCain for supposedly "siring" an illegitimate black child, who in fact was his adopted Bangladeshi daughter.

Democrats Jimmy Carter and Bill Clinton also were the beneficiaries, in effect if not in intention, of a "Southern Strategy lite." Both were white Southerners, and Carter was an evangelical Christian. Clinton made a point of repudiating extreme, anti-white remarks made by the hip-hop artist Sister Souljah, and flew home to Arkansas, where he was then the Governor, to prove his "tough on crime" bona fides by overseeing the execution of Ricky Ray Rector.

Still, while the Republican candidates exploited racial bias and the Democrats at least benefited from it, the two parties shared a rough consensus about ethnic tolerance and economic centrism.

Meanwhile, despite recessions and interest rate spikes, the curve of postwar prosperity continued steeply upward. In parallel, the Soviet Union and the Eastern Bloc declined, and then suddenly collapsed. In 1989, the Berlin Wall fell.

Based on the resounding success of the post-World War II Western order, political scientist Francis Fukuyama judged in 1992 that the world had reached *The End of History*: we had arrived at the optimal combination of politics and economics: liberal democracy combined with regulated free markets.[62]

Some moderate Republicans and moderate Democrats began to find that they had more in common with each other than they did with the partisan bases of their own parties. Clinton's 1992 campaign was a production of the Democratic Leadership Council, a centrist, pro-business group with a mission to reform the Democratic Party after what were seen as the leftward excesses of the late sixties. In 2000, George W. Bush campaigned on "compassionate conservatism," which pursued traditionally conservative economic ends alongside ethnic inclusivity and support for selected social programs.

By then, the meeting-in-the-middle seemed to have created a Coke-Pepsi choice between the two major parties: the differences came down to relatively minor matters of preference. On the left, taxes were a little higher and regulations a little stricter; on the right, a little less so. And that looked to be about it.

We were so innocent then.

In retrospect, we can see that moderate Democrats and Republicans had formed a virtual third party, composed of well-educated urbanites who were living in an imaginary world where the civic nationalist map still represented reality. Floating in their cloud city, they were oblivious to what was going on in the ethnic territory below.

They were winners in the global boom, which they boosted further with global trade deals like NAFTA, the North American Free Trade Agreement. The rising tide would lift all boats, as John F. Kennedy had said.[63] It was certainly lifting theirs.

Culturally, they were multi: they found common interests with people like themselves across America and across the world. Clinton-like leaders were elected in other Western countries, notably in the UK, where Tony Blair's New Labor mirrored Clinton's New Democrats. In the US, some of the moderately liberal members of the "third party" founded an organization called Third Way, which is still active.

But although "globalist" was a term of pride and hope in the cloud city, on the ground it was becoming a dirty word, used with a varying mix of economic or cultural anxiety and bigotry, depending on the situation and the speaker. Again, it was hard to untangle race and culture. Calling someone a "globalist" might be a critique of stateless international finance, or "globalist" might just be code for "Jew," as similar terms were for Wagner and many of his contemporaries.

Similarly, the "New World Order" that had been hailed by George H.W. Bush was now seen as a dark conspiracy. Maybe it was being run by the UN or some other international cabal, and maybe that cabal was ultimately run by Jews. At ground level, what many people saw were jobs flowing out of the country, immigrants flowing in, and money flowing to "elites" who were loyal to no country.

At the top of society the traditional, horizontal divide between left and right appeared to be closing. But there was a new, and growing, vertical divide, between the moderate, multicultural, technocratic, bipartisan elite, and an increasingly angry, Euro-American middle and bottom: the populist right. The latter saw themselves, for the first time, as an underclass.

A Virtual Secession

T he vertical divide was deepened further by new forms of media: talk radio, cable and satellite TV, and then the Internet. Sharp-eyed entrepreneurs like Rush Limbaugh, Nixon veteran Roger Ailes, Matt Drudge, and Andrew Breitbart spotted a business opportunity in the anger of cultural conservatives who felt unrepresented in or even insulted by mainstream news coverage. The new media entrepreneurs exploited that feeling by leveraging the same electronic technology that was boosting the globalized economy. Some of them were also helped by the 1987 termination of broadcasting's Fairness Doctrine, which since 1949 had required broadcasters, though never cable TV networks, to present opposing views on controversial issues.

At first dismissed as a fringe phenomenon, right-wing media became hugely successful. Fox News went from no TV presence in its headquarters city of New York to dominance of cable ratings across the country.

Right-wing news outlets didn't only attract a big new audience, though. They repelled consumers of traditional news, who were shocked by what they saw as opinion masquerading as journalism, opinion that was focused on sensation, conspiracy theories, and cultural and racial resentment.

That split remains. But to see Fox News and the rest as simply a corruption of traditional journalism is not entirely accurate: Fox, for example, does have a legitimate news operation along with the prime-time opinion programming that draws most of the attention. Moreover, there's a larger point: with Fox News, Roger Ailes and owner Rupert Murdoch *rejected* the traditional model of journalism and built an alternative.

It was another battle in the war of Counter-Enlightenment vs. Enlightenment worldviews. Journalist Gabriel Sherman describes Ailes' and Murdoch's strategy in his deeply reported Ailes biography, *The Loudest Voice in the Room:*

> Together, Murdoch and Ailes were embarking on a holy
> mission to lay waste to smug journalistic standards. "We will
> be the insurgents in a business of very strong incumbents,"
> Murdoch said shortly after hiring Ailes. He spoke of "a
> growing disconnect between television news and its audience,"
> and "an increasing gap between the values of those that deliver
> the news and those that receive it."[64]

While working for the 1968 Nixon campaign, Ailes had realized that news and politics could be packaged as entertainment. That approach showed up everywhere on Fox News, from the emotional intensity of the stories to the flashy graphics, long since copied by nearly all cable news channels.

Bill Clinton was a perfect bad guy for Fox's news-entertainment narratives. To cultural conservatives, Clinton embodied everything they had hated about the sixties: a slick, pot-smoking, draft-dodging, pro-choice libertine, with a wife who seemed to think just keeping a home was beneath her. The Monica Lewinsky scandal was a gift to Fox News, boosting ratings by 400 percent. It was a perfect collision of cultures, as Sherman recounts:

> "The Lewinsky story did for Fox News what Fox News
> couldn't do for itself," a former producer in the Washington
> bureau said. The combination of sex and schadenfreude
> generated massive ratings at a fraction of the cost of a foreign
> crisis. "Monica [Lewinsky] was a news channel's dream come
> true," [Fox executive] John Moody said. "It was cheap in both
> senses." It was during this period that Fox's prime-time stars,
> Bill O'Reilly and Sean Hannity among them, were reborn as
> cultural bulwarks against a growing number of contemptible
> influences: Bill Clinton's libido, the media, environmentalists,
> gay activists, you name it.[65]

At launch, Fox News had two now-familiar slogans: "We report, you decide" and "Fair and balanced." Both expressed Ailes' and Murdoch's belief that a liberal worldview was embedded in the media's supposedly objective news. But

"We report, you decide" also represented a subtle but significant shift from Enlightenment objectivity to Counter-Enlightenment subjectivity. On one level it simply asserted that Fox would *not* mix opinion with news. But on another, it transferred editorial responsibility — the determination of truth — from journalists to consumers.

In the previous era of journalism, Walter Cronkite could sign off with his authoritative "And that's the way it is." Ailes and Murdoch were saying, in effect, "Not necessarily."

The media personalities of Fox News and other right-wing outlets would stand up for their audience against liberals, globalists, intellectuals, Hollywood, and the elites. All of those were shown as arrogant, immoral, and unpatriotic: seeking to turn America into Europe, or worse, Russia (until recently, that is, given that Putin's Russia is now ethnonationalist, and seen by many Trump supporters as an ally in the anti-globalist resistance).

It sold. Whereas formerly the money was in mass media, now fortunes could be made in niche media, which served people only what they wanted to see — while claiming it was what the elites *didn't* want them to see.

Fox News profited the most from the Clinton-Lewinsky scandal and sensations to follow, but CNN and MSNBC ended up following that lead, too, though from the ideological middle and left. Both have seen some of their highest ratings during the scandal-a-day Trump administration. Trump often highlights the debt they owe his instinct for drawing eyeballs.[66]

As niche media won more and more of the audience from mainstream media, one of the safeguards built into American democracy began to dissolve.

Montesquieu had predicted that a democratic republic would be endangered by the formation of factions. He argued for the separation of powers (a concept dating back to the ancient Roman Republic) to protect against factionalism within government. To prevent factions forming among the people, he believed that the republic must be small, so that its population would be homogeneous.

James Madison agreed with Montesquieu about the threat posed by factions, warning in *Federalist* Number 10 that "democracies have ever been spectacles of turbulence and contention… and have in general been as short in their lives as they have been violent in their deaths."[67]

But Madison believed that as America grew, its size would *protect* it against factions. He thought factionalists would have difficulty communicating and coordinating with each other across a large territory, and so would end up contending with and balancing each other. In *Federalist* 10, Madison went on to explain that "The influence of factious leaders may kindle a flame within their particular States, but will be unable to spread a general conflagration through the other States."[68]

What Madison didn't foresee was that not just factionalism, but sectionalism would threaten the union. Conflict over the spread of slavery pushed the civic and ethnic nations further apart, even as the country grew.

And Madison couldn't have foreseen how distance would shrink in a world of electronic media. First, radio and TV enabled instantaneous communication at any distance. Then the Internet eliminated the barrier to coordination.

The rise of niche media enabled like-minded people to form factions that spanned the continent. As media entrepreneurs chased a market segment, a media bubble would form around that audience. People of different cultures began to inhabit different media realities, producing a virtual sectionalism.

This trend was amplified by others outside the bubbles, in physical reality. Cheap transportation, telecommunications, and climate control made it feasible for more Americans to live where they wanted. It turned out to be among people like themselves. That could have been predicted, given sociological research on homophily, the tendency of "birds of a feather to flock together."[69] Journalist Bill Bishop documented a nationwide homophilic trend in *The Big Sort* (2008):

> People don't live in states. They live in communities. And those communities are not close to being in equipoise, even within solidly blue or red states. They are, most of them, becoming even more Democratic or Republican. As Americans have moved over the past three decades, they have clustered in communities of sameness, among people with similar ways of life, beliefs, and, in the end, politics. Little, if any, of this political migration was by design, a conscious effort by people to live among like-voting neighbors. When my wife and I moved to Austin, we didn't go hunting for the most Democratic neighborhood in town. But the result was the same: moving to Travis Heights, we took a side and fell into a stark geographic

pattern of political belief, one that has grown more distinct in presidential elections since 1976.

Over the past thirty years, the United States has been sorting itself, sifting at the most microscopic levels of society… When people move, they also make choices about who their neighbors will be and who will share their new lives. Those are now political decisions, and they are having a profound effect on the nation's public life.[70]

These media and real-world trends weakened political parties, by loosening their control over information and organization. Now, party members could connect at will with content and with each other.

For a while, though, the Republican Party only gained, especially from the right-wing media firing up voters on the GOP's behalf.

But then the Republicans discovered the truth of what Winston Churchill said about riding a tiger: the tiger may eat you.[71] Since the sixties, Republican politicians had been riding their angry, culturally conservative base into office by *talking* about abortion, welfare, gays, guns, and God. But once elected, what they *did* was cut taxes and regulations for rich people and corporations.

It was pretty neat, while it lasted. Previously, the GOP had faced a fundamental math problem: there aren't as many rich voters as non-rich ones. But now they had found a way to get labor to vote for the interests of capital.

As right-wing media took off, things just got better and better for conservative pols. But then the base became able to talk to each other across the country. Comparing notes, they started to figure out the game their own party's elite had been running on them.

We're Throwing
Our Own Party

A lthough Bill Clinton was succeeded by a Republican, the populist right's suspicion and anger would grow during the George W. Bush administration. Bush's aggressive response to the 9/11 attack temporarily won him overwhelming base support, but that faded as the wars in Afghanistan and Iraq went so wrong, at terribly asymmetric cost to working people and their families. Then a deregulated Wall Street crashed the economy — again pushing the suffering down the social hierarchy, while those at the top got bailed out.

Shortly after Barack Obama took office in January of 2009, the Tea Party shot to national prominence, seemingly propelled by an explosion of long-building populist fury triggered by the crash. At around the same time, a technology-enabled, grassroots movement developed on the left as well — the "netroots." It grew up around online organizing platforms like MoveOn.org (created in 1998 in response to the impeachment of Bill Clinton), progressive blogs like Daily Kos, and the tech-savvy Howard Dean presidential campaign of 2004.

But while the anger on the right was no doubt real, the Tea Party was artificially enhanced: much of its grassroots activism was actually "Astroturf," generously funded by the libertarian billionaires the Koch Brothers and their allies. Jane Mayer of *The New Yorker* wrote a definitive study of such hidden-hand political organizing, *Dark Money (2016)*. Mayer traced the Tea Party's engineered origins:

In 1991, [the Koch-funded nonprofit] Citizens for a Sound
Economy promoted what was advertised as a massive "re-
enactment of the Boston Tea Party" in Raleigh, North Carolina,
to protest tax increases. Among those present, the press corps
nearly outnumbered the clutch of protesters in Revolutionary
War, Uncle Sam, and Santa Claus costumes. The following
year, Citizens for a Sound Economy was involved in another
plan to stage a Tea Party protest. This one was secretly funded
by tobacco companies to fight cigarette taxes and was canceled
after its covert funding was exposed. By 2007, Citizens for a
Sound Economy had split up. The Kochs' new organization,
Americans for Prosperity, tried to stage another Tea Party
protest against taxes, this time in Texas. It too was a dud.
Nonetheless, by the time Obama was elected and the economy
was melting down, the rudiments of a political machine were in
place, along with a network of paid operatives expert in
creating colonially garbed "Astroturf" groups to fake the
appearance of public support.[72]

On Feb. 18, 2009, the newly-elected President Obama introduced the
Homeowners Affordability and Stability Plan. It was designed to help millions
of homeowners avoid foreclosure, including many Tea Party supporters. But then
CNBC reporter Rick Santelli delivered an apparently spontaneous live rant on
the floor of the Chicago Mercantile Exchange. Santelli painted a very different
picture of relief for homeowners: undeserving others being bailed out by Big
Government.

The government is promoting bad behavior! How is this,
president and new administration, why didn't you put up a
website to have people vote on the Internet as a referendum to
see if we really want to subsidize the losers' mortgages; or,
would we like to at least buy cars and buy houses in
foreclosure and give 'em to people that might have a chance to
actually prosper down the road and reward people that could
carry the water instead of drink the water. This is America!
How many of you people want to pay for your neighbor's
mortgage that has an extra bathroom and can't pay their bills?
Raise their hand. [Boos from traders in the background.]
President Obama, are you listening?[73]

Those traders cheering in the background were members of the same economic and professional class that had just screwed the Tea Partiers. It didn't matter, at least partly because so much of the fury was cultural and/or racial. A website appeared almost immediately, and Tea Party protests broke out across the country.

Mobilization at that scale was made possible by the Kochs and other billionaires.

This tiger carried the Kochs a long way, and still does, as Mayer documents. *Dark Money* tracks the Kochs' continuing influence throughout the Trump administration, the Republican Congress, and the 50 states.

But the tiger ate the GOP. During the two terms of the Obama administration, old-guard Republicans like John Boehner and Paul Ryan tried mightily to balance on the tiger's back, but fell one by one. They were replaced by hard-core right-wing partisans like Michelle Bachman, Jim Jordan, Mark Meadows, Kevin McCarthy, and Mick Mulvaney (recently one of a series of Chiefs of Staff for President Trump). Then Trump won the nomination against fragmented opposition, and Trumpism took over the GOP.

As the Senate impeachment trial made clear, the Republican Party now stands for a single person, not principles independent of person. It is now an entirely Counter-Enlightenment institution.

When Everyone Is
Out to Get You

A lthough the right-wing media were new, their populist message was not. That, too, can be traced to the 18th and 19th century origins of the Counter-Enlightenment.

In his 2002 study *Enemies of the Enlightenment,* historian Darrin McMahon documents an extensive literature of contemporaneous attacks on the Enlightenment, both from on high and from a "Grub Street" media that prefigured today's right-wing tabloids. Allowing for changes in diction, much of it could have been written today:

> If the destruction of religion was thus seen as an explicit goal and an inherent result of the teachings of the *philosophes,* one that threatened society on a vast scale, their opponents viewed this horrific outcome as both cause and effect of another of *philosophie's* pernicious consequences: the corruption of social morals. At the most basic level, anti-*philosophes* argued that by eliminating the fear of God and an afterlife, breaching the ramparts of Christian morality, and destroying respect for religious authority, the *philosophes* removed all impediments to humanity's basest tendencies... "What have we seen as a result of this so-called century of lights but a frightening inundation of every sort of crime — impiety, injustice, cruelty, libertinage, deception, fraud, and suicide?" asked the Dominican Barthelemi Baudrand in what would prove to be an extremely popular work of anti-*philosophe* piety. In his similarly successful anti-*philosophe* novel, Les Helviennes, the abbe Barruel charged that the "natural effect" of the *philosophes'* writings was to create "monsters," who could be

seen at every level of society, from the grands down to the "brigand who lays his traps for travelers in the isolation of the forest, or the valet who assassinates his master in the shadow of night." Having imbibed the teachings of the *philosophes,* these men were restrained by no moral restrictions, only by fear of punishment.[74]

The conspiratorial thinking seen here proved to be a durable feature of the Counter-Enlightenment. Over time it has discerned shadowy schemes among Jews, Papists, Freemasons, bohemians, homosexuals, crypto-communists, crypto-fascists, water fluoridators, whoever "really" killed JFK, the United Nations, the Illuminati, the Bilderberg Group, the Skull and Bones Society, alien abductors, Bill and Hillary Clinton, the "true" 9/11 attackers, Barack and Michelle Obama, George Soros, "chemtrail" generators, vaccine manufacturers, round earth hoaxers, climate scientists, the "Deep State," and the Satan-worshipping pedophiles we are warned of by QAnon.

In a landmark 1964 *Harper's Magazine* article, historian Richard Hofstader identified "The Paranoid Style in American Politics:"

> I believe there is a style of mind that is far from new and that is not necessarily right-wing. I call it the paranoid style simply because no other word adequately evokes the sense of heated exaggeration, suspiciousness, and conspiratorial fantasy that I have in mind. In using the expression "paranoid style" I am not speaking in a clinical sense, but borrowing a clinical term for other purposes. I have neither the competence nor the desire to classify any figures of the past or present as certifiable lunatics. In fact, the idea of the paranoid style as a force in politics would have little contemporary relevance or historical value if it were applied only to men with profoundly disturbed minds. It is the use of paranoid modes of expression by more or less normal people that makes the phenomenon significant.[75]

In 2013, historian Michael Barkun defined what he called "stigmatized knowledge" in his book *A Culture of Conspiracy.* He based the concept on James Webb's "rejected knowledge" (in *The Occult Establishment,* 1976) and Colin Campbell's "cultic milieu" (in *The Cultic Milieu: Oppositional Subcultures in an Age of Globalization,* 2002). An excerpt from Barkun:

Christianity, in the course of achieving cultural hegemony, suppressed or ignored bodies of belief deemed to be irrelevant, erroneous, or outmoded. By the same token, those whose beliefs seem to conflict with dominant values sometimes choose to withdraw into subcultural undergrounds. The result is the creation of worldviews that exist in opposition to the prevailing ones and manifest in such forms as "Spiritualism, Theosophy, countless Eastern (and not so Eastern) cults; varieties of Christian sectarianism and the esoteric pursuits of magic, alchemy and astrology; also the pseudosciences."

Such underground worldviews tend to be ill-defined potpourris in which are "jumbled together the droppings of all cultures, and occasional fragments of philosophy perhaps profound but almost certainly subversive to right living in the society in which the believer finds himself." This cultural dumping ground of the heretical, the scandalous, the unfashionable, and the dangerous received renewed interest in the nineteenth century, when at least some in the West became bored or disillusioned with rationalism. Such ideas were often presented under the rubric of "ancient wisdom" — the alleged recovery of a body of knowledge from the remote past supposedly superior to the scientific and rational knowledge more recently acquired.[76]

As with other forms of content, the spread of conspiracy theories has been accelerated by technology, starting with the invention of writing and continuing through the printing press, postal services, radio, and TV, then accelerating to the hyperbolic growth rate we've seen since the invention of the Internet.

Enter the Demagogue

A s the reach and impact of conspiracy theories has risen with the growth of technology, so too has the potential power of demagogues, casting themselves as the people's only hope against dark, alien threats.

Demagogues have always been with us, but only with the arrival of radio, film, and then TV did we see them rise as fast and as far as a Lenin, Hitler, Mussolini, or Mao. Even in 1917, Lenin knew he would want a radio within earshot of every citizen of the Soviet Union, and he made sure millions of cheap sets were produced.

With today's technology, a demagogue can gather conspiracy theories from anywhere, including his imaginings of the moment, and instantaneously beam them into minds everywhere. Since many of those minds already think within a conspiratorial framework, the content of the conspiracy may not matter, as long as it feels right. Evidence to the contrary hardly matters either, since it can always be countered with "That's what *they* want you to believe" — and "they" can be almost anyone, since they live in the shadows. Neither does the content matter much to the demagogue, as long as it undermines faith in institutions and objective data, and scares up support for "the only one you can trust."

Trump is a classic demagogue. Alexander Hamilton thought the Electoral College would protect us from someone like this making it to the presidency, but it turns out Hamilton was wrong when he wrote this in *Federalist* 68:

> The process of election affords a moral certainty, that the office
> of President will never fall to the lot of any man who is not in
> an eminent degree endowed with the requisite qualifications.
> Talents for low intrigue, and the little arts of popularity, may
> alone suffice to elevate a man to the first honors in a single

State; but it will require other talents, and a different kind of
merit, to establish him in the esteem and confidence of the
whole Union, or of so considerable a portion of it as would be
necessary to make him a successful candidate for the
distinguished office of President of the United States. It will
not be too strong to say, that there will be a constant probability
of seeing the station filled by characters pre-eminent for ability
and virtue.[77]

Trump founded his career on the racist birther conspiracy theory, which
falsely asserted that Barack Obama was really born in Kenya. He has exploited
one conspiracy after another ever since, stoking fear of Muslim immigrants,
Latino immigrants, immigrants from "shithole countries," the "fake news" as
"the enemy of the people," the "Deep State," and even America's own law
enforcement, intelligence, and military services. All of them, according to
Trump, are arrayed against him and therefore against his people.

That identification with the people is crucial. An effective demagogue has a
deep, if often instinctive, grasp of symbolism. Not only does the demagogue
promise to ease his followers' suffering, he promises to take that suffering on.
He presents daily life as a drama in which he is both the people's only champion
and the primary victim of their enemies. This is why Trump's constant
complaining about being treated unfairly, even though he holds the most
powerful office in the world, doesn't make him look weak in the eyes of his
followers: he is suffering, Messiah-like, so they won't have to.

The mockery of Trump by his critics can boost the power of this symbol. As
we saw with the Fisher King, the Messiah can take many forms. One is the clown,
who suffers humiliation on behalf of the audience. Trump is frequently insulted
as a clown, and with his improbable hair, orange makeup, overlong ties,
exaggerated gestures and facial expressions, and frequent, unembarrassed
displays of incompetence, he almost seems to be inviting it. At some level, he
may be. Demagogues often have clownish aspects. But since the demagogue is
powerful and vengeful, he can also promise that Judgment Day is coming for
those who mock him and his followers.

Through identification with their followers, the most effective demagogues
have been able to turn popular democracies into populist personality cults. The

institutions of government no longer belong to the public, but to the demagogue, personally, claiming to act on the public's behalf, or rather, *as* the public.

The rise of a demagogue is the return of the king.

Part II

What's Happening Now

Trump Was Inevitable

Donald Trump's victory on Nov. 8, 2016 astonished most of the world — starting with him, according to several sources, including his former "fixer," Michael Cohen.[78] Apparently, Trump had planned that date as the end of a brand-building project, not the beginning of a presidency.

But the election of Trump, or someone like him, sooner or later, has been inevitable since July 4, 1776.

One of the more startling statements made by Trump supporters is that this most unabashedly profane of men has been anointed by God.[79] It's the kind of thing that makes Trump opponents wonder if half the country either has gone insane, or is trying to cause insanity by gaslighting.

Trump as the Chosen One makes no rational sense, but as we began to explore in the previous chapter, it makes all kinds of non-rational sense, in the context of America's parallel, Counter-Enlightenment history.

Trump is that history's fulfillment. Every strand comes together in him.

Count the ways:

1. His ethnic nationalism and xenophobia.
2. His rejection of reason and science in favor of emotion and intuition.
3. His use of symbols and assertions of belief in place of facts and rational arguments.
4. His conversion of himself into a symbol, an apotheosis from Donald Trump the person to the gilded, omnipresent Trump brand.
5. His resentment of elites, experts, and all who might somehow look down on him and his followers.
6. His mastery of media and celebrity.
7. His conspiratorial paranoia.

8. His monarchical view of how government works, seeing its organs as his: "my military," "my Attorney General," etc.

9. His narcissism. With his constant need for attention and immediate gratification, and tantrums when he doesn't get them, it's hard to look at Trump and not think of His Majesty the Baby.

10. And his role as a Messiah: he identifies himself with the people, he suffers on their behalf, he claims to perform miracles, and he promises a restored paradise in an America made "great again."

It's all there, in Trump. He's perfect for this moment.

He speaks to people whose reality is built not on reason, but on faith. Not deduction, but intuition. Not research, but revelation. Not words, but images. Not society, but nature. Not science, but culture. Not facts, but what they see as higher truths.

Much of America, more than many of us ever knew, lives in this reality, and always has. It's just become more visible in recent decades. Bob Dole saw, and tried to ride, the insurgency on the 1988 presidential campaign trail, as he ran, unsuccessfully, for the Republican nomination. In Ames, Iowa Dole had to follow a roof-raising speech by evangelist and rival candidate Pat Robertson. Richard Ben Cramer captured the experience in his classic account of the '88 campaign, *What It Takes:*

> Dole knew why these people didn't look like Republicans, why they'd never shown up in any crowd before. Dole never needed a writer to tell him how to talk to the dispossessed. These people were left-outs. (That's why they were watching Robertson's TV show!) ... The message Bob Dole left with them, that Saturday, was simple: they mattered to him. That was the day when Dole got the endorsement of Iowa's Senator Grassley ("Chuckeeee!") ... and it was Grassley who introduced him, with the phrase that summed it up in one line. "He's one of us!" Grassley said. That line stuck with Dole. It was perfect for Iowa—for everyplace (and everyone) left out of Reagan's shower of gold. It linked Dole — in four words! — with the millions (these God-struck folk at Ames, for example) who felt that Washington was a place cut off from their town, from their lives, from the values they held dear.[80]

These are the people of Trump's base today, overjoyed to finally have a leader who sees things the way they do, who speaks to them. That's the source of the exultation at Trump's rallies: here at long last, is the one *they* have been waiting for. He tells them *their* nation is *the* nation, separate, and better.

This is a map of the Divided States of America, following the 2016 presidential election:

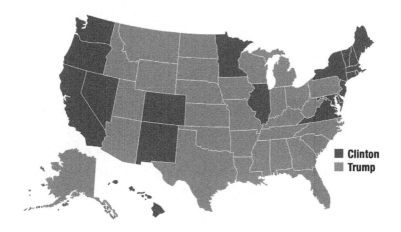

This is the America we live in now, whether or not we want to.

The United States of America was a promised land we promised ourselves. But we never made it there.

Liberals: Good at Economics,
Bad at Culture

T
he Enlightenment's rationalists believed, like Jefferson with his Bible, that they could substitute the clarity of reason for the mysteries of faith. They thought a social contract could replace culture. They were wrong. Once a culture is rooted, philosophy isn't likely to root it out. George Orwell told us this back in 1941, in his essay "The Lion and the Unicorn," written as England was under bombardment by the Nazis, although few rationalists then grasped the importance of his words:

> The intellectuals who hope to see [England] Russianised or Germanised will be disappointed. The gentleness, the hypocrisy, the thoughtlessness, the reverence for law and the hatred of uniforms will remain, along with the suet puddings and the misty skies. It needs some very great disaster, such as prolonged subjugation by a foreign enemy, to destroy a national culture. The Stock Exchange will be pulled down, the horse plough will give way to the tractor, the country houses will be turned into children's holiday camps, the Eton and Harrow match will be forgotten, but England will still be England, an everlasting animal stretching into the future and the past, and, like all living things, having the power to change out of recognition and yet remain the same.[81]

Orwell knew that almost all British subjects, even with their many regional and class divisions, saw themselves as Britons — who "never, never, never will be slaves," as they sang in their hymn to the goddess Britannia. Britons didn't just work and pay taxes under one system or another. Britons would go down fighting rather than surrender their land and culture. It was Britons whom Churchill addressed when he swore that "we shall fight on the beaches, we shall fight on the landing grounds, we shall fight in the fields and in the streets, we shall fight in the hills; we shall never surrender."[82]

I suspect neither Churchill nor Orwell would be surprised by Brexit.

The sleeping nationalism of the British was awakened in World War II by an existential threat. The threats faced by modern Americans are far less serious and are exaggerated by right-wing politicians and media. Nevertheless, many Euro-Americans believe that their culture is in mortal danger. Some of them are bigots, but some are not, or at least not intentionally so. The latter want to preserve their culture not because they hate other ones, but because they love their own.

We are social beings. That phrase is such a commonplace that we can miss its full, and deep, meaning: *our being is social.* Alone, we are vulnerable and miserable. We require the company of others. We need culture.

A trip through MAGA country reveals that in person, many Trump voters are honest, kind, and generous, like so many other Americans are. They see their culture, like most people do, as an important source of their own best qualities. It's hard to reconcile images of screaming MAGA fans at a Trump rally and the same people in real life. But bear in mind that Trump, like every demagogue, presents himself as their only protector against cultural decay and destruction: he summons their worst instincts — instincts that, as Freud would remind us, lurk in us all.

When political liberals see *all* resistance to cultural change as bigotry, they miss how frightening change can look. Trump supporters have been convinced that liberals want to destroy their culture. Culture is a human need, linked to survival, and fear for one's survival has nothing to do with reason.

Liberals' cultural blind spot explains much about how the Democratic Party has lost the white working-class part of its base. It also explains its alienation of some black and brown people.

Consider the claim by progressives that the "Democratic establishment" rigged the 2020 primaries for the moderate Joe Biden. This charge is not only wrong, but insulting to the voters Democrats need most in order to win.

Biden's campaign was saved in the Feb. 29 South Carolina primary by mostly African-American, working- and middle-class voters, with a huge assist from a trusted local leader, Rep. Jim Clyburn. Otherwise, Biden would have lost, or, possibly, squeezed out a disappointingly narrow win. He would not have seen the cascade of support he got on Monday, March 2. The next day, Super Tuesday, he won other states thanks to a lot of other working- and middle-class voters, again with strong support from African Americans.

The willingness to believe the "establishment" narrative is a key reason why Democrats lose elections they should win. The narrative depends on the mistaken belief, going all the way back to Marx and still hanging on even among people who don't think of themselves as Marxists, that everything is explained by economics: there's a monolithic working class and its economic struggle against the capitalist class is what drives politics and history.

But if Marx had lived long enough to meet Freud, he might have realized that while there is a working class when it comes to some shared economic interests, class identity evaporates when it comes to behavior. Instead, there are millions and millions of individuals who have complex, often irrational psyches, and who are members of widely variable cultures, which are built of symbols and rituals, not facts and logic.

I'd guess, for example, that many on the left would be surprised to learn that even though an overwhelming majority of African Americans are Democrats, only about a quarter identify as liberals.[83]

When actual human beings make choices, as opposed to the rational actors of classical economics, culture frequently trumps economics — as it did in the choice of Trump. His cultural representation is as the defender of the little guy. The economic reality is corporate and capital gains tax cuts, deregulation, a cabinet stocked with corporate lobbyists, and a knack for using government resources for his own benefit. It's a time-tested bait and switch, well known to, for example, shady real estate promoters: distract 'em with emotion, screw 'em with numbers.

Democrats get economics right and culture wrong. Despite the conventional wisdom, Democratic administrations have generally out-performed Republican ones in economic results for all classes.[84] But blindness to the power of culture often leaves Democrats scratching their heads after elections, wondering what just happened to them — again. They ask themselves questions like *What's the Matter With Kansas?*[85]

Immanuel Kant argued that as far as we know, reality is chaos, filtered into order by our perceptions. For progressives, the filter is economics.

What's the matter with Kansas is that a lot of white working-class people who used to vote Democratic stopped doing that because of culture.

And more black and brown people might too, if they keep having the experience of being overlooked, taken for granted, or outright insulted.

Culture & Soul

Even without insulting people, liberals often have trouble connecting with them, because many liberals are hard to connect *with*. They can and should be proud of standing up for equality and inclusion, and for accepting the political cost of having made racists unwelcome in their party. But along the way liberals, like other Enlightenment rationalists, seem to have deracinated themselves. By standing for all cultures, they come across as belonging to none.

This can make them less effective communicators, because communication requires trust.

When one electronic device connects to another, it begins with what's called a "handshake." This is an exchange of digital bits, by which the devices identify what they are, what kind of language they understand, and what they can do.

This is modeled after what people do when they meet — except people aren't machines! People don't exchange data to establish trust, they exchange symbols and perform rituals — like, for example, a physical handshake. There's no data in a handshake, just feeling.

Now let's think about what happens when two stiff, over-thinking Enlightenment types meet — I feel I can talk like this about them because I am, more or less, one of these people — as compared with people who come from a more soulful culture, one that has elements of the Counter-Enlightenment still active within it.

People from soulful cultures have a repertoire of introductory facial expressions, phrases, sounds, and moves that they habitually perform. None of these may make "sense," but all of them are rich in meaning. Enlightenment people are more "Hi. How are you." All content, no connection.

You know this is true. It's why cultural "fish out of water" contrasts are such comedy evergreens: the awkward white guy in the dance club, the greenhorn on a horse, the Anglo-Saxon tourist in Italy. Yes, they're stereotypes, but stereotypes don't come from nowhere.

I have been all of these characters.

I was in Rome recently. A local asked me how I liked it. "It's wonderful," I said, as enthusiastically as I could manage, because I really meant it.

His face lit up, his voice rose like song, and with his whole body, he exulted, "I LOOOOOOOVE THIS CITY! I was BORN here, and I'm gonna DIE HERE!!!"

It was like he was the opera, and I was the playbill. He's why people like me love Italy, and will pay a lot of money to be there, if only for a little while.

People like me also love Hawaii, not just because of the beauty and the weather, but because of the culture. Like many visitors to the islands, I've been struck by the story of how we came to be called *haoles*. It's quite possibly apocryphal, but it sure *feels* true.

The "ha" syllable in *haole* is also found in the beautiful greeting *Aloha*. *Ha* refers to the breath, which symbolizes both life and the soul. When two traditional Hawaiians met, they would move close together, so that their noses could touch, and they could share breath. Newcomers to the island (many of whom were missionaries who thought much of Hawaiian culture was inappropriate or sinful) didn't do this. So they were called *haoles,* because it means "without breath."[86]

Soulless. But we *haoles* keep coming, looking for that same breath of soul. History repeats, first as invasion and then as tourism.

The same kind of disconnect happens whenever Enlightenment Americans and Counter-Enlightenment Americans meet. Thinking of Trump supporters, we might translate "liberal" as Kansan for *haole*.

In some ways, Hawaii reminds me of Bermuda, where my father was born and where I grew up from the age of 13. Our family moved there from Canada. Canada is a wonderful place, but I'm pretty sure few Canadians would argue with me when I say that Canadians, especially the ones descended from the British Isles, are, shall we say, restrained. Bermudians, especially when I lived there, were not. For me, the transition from Canada to Bermuda was something like what happens in *The Wizard of Oz,* when Dorothy opens the door of her family's Kansas farmhouse. Black and white switched to Technicolor.

Growing up in Bermuda meant that I learned new ways of seeing, thinking, feeling, and communicating, through the different cultures that came together on those tiny, isolated islands, from Great Britain, West Africa, the Caribbean, Portugal, and the United States. I'm forever grateful.

The Enlightenment legacy of reason is a precious gift. But relying only on reason constricts us. When it comes to communication, it's as if we were using a telegraph to tap out letters, instead of TV to broadcast images and sound.

Consider "Don't Mess With Texas." It's one of the most successful social marketing campaigns in history. It was created by Austin-based ad agency GSD&M, after the State of Texas had failed for years to persuade Texans to stop littering. Agency co-founder Tim McClure realized that a big part of the problem was the use of the word "litter." The story was told in the January, 2011 issue of *Texas Monthly:*

> Research showed that the main culprits were young truck-driving males, and McClure needed a catchphrase that would grab their attention.
>
> "I was up before dawn one day, walking outside and racking my brains for the right words," recalls McClure, who grew up in East Texas. "As I was walking, I noticed that even the sides of the road in my nice neighborhood were piled with trash. It made me mad. That's when it hit me: Texans wouldn't call this litter. The only time I'd ever used the word 'litter' was with puppies and kittens. Instead I was reminded of what my mom used to say about my room growing up. Real Texans would call this a mess.
>
> Almost immediately, four simple words — "Don't mess with Texas" — coalesced in his mind, and a battle cry was born. Since then, the phrase has become embedded in the collective psyche not just of Texans but of the whole country.[87]

When Texans heard "Please don't litter," they heard a non-Texan — maybe even an *Easterner* — trying to tell them what to do. And progress stopped right there.

But when iconic Texans like Willie Nelson or members of the Dallas Cowboys said, "Don't mess with Texas," that made all the difference. While littering had been persistent, messing with Texas plummeted.

When Trump fans hear him say "Make America Great Again," they either don't hear his bigoted subtext, or they choose to ignore it. They hear, or choose to hear, someone promising to protect and restore their culture.

In rightly resisting the xenophobic aspect of MAGA, liberals deploy the losing tactic of trying to replace something — in this case a culture — with what by comparison feels like nothing — information.

That's what's often behind cultural conservatives' dislike of liberals. In place of a cultural home, liberals seem to offer only alienation, the curse of the tree of Enlightenment knowledge.

If people fear that they're losing their culture, they need reassurance, not just explanations of why they're wrong. Yes, their anxiety is often groundless — many red state residents have the least amount of contact with other cultures.[88]

But beliefs trump facts — like culture trumps reason.

And thus Trump.

Poetry, Magic & Amusement

T o his most committed followers, it makes no difference when Trump makes no sense. In fact, not making sense can be the point, when the enemy is seen as both relentlessly sense-making and spiritually empty. Trump gives his audience not logical arguments, but the connection-making exchange of symbols and ritual they hunger for. And if he drives liberal rationalists crazy too, that's a big bonus.

Instead of developing political arguments, Trump creates and repeats brand names: Fake News, Deep State, Witch Hunt, Russia Hoax, Crooked Hillary, Sham Impeachment.

Short, rhythmic brand phrases are a form of poetry, one of our most ancient forms of encoding culture — and of defining reality. Poetry has roots in magical incantation.

As skilled marketers, politicians, actors, and hypnotists know, to use language is always to cast a kind of spell. Enlightenment rationalists, focused on information, tend to overlook the power of language as sound apart from meaning. Their own diction is often stripped of emotion, except, perhaps, when safely wrapped in air quotes.

But whether or not we're consciously aware of it, the sound of language acts on all of us all day long, shaping our experiences, emotions, and decisions.

As Trump knows both professionally and personally, a crucial dimension of marketing any product is the sound of its brand name. The way such names are designed gives the lie to the conventional wisdom that studying poetry is a ticket to unemployment. Branding is big business, amounting to billions of dollars in equity for some corporations. Much of that value is contained in the way a brand name sounds.

For example, it's no accident that so many brand names feature "k" sounds. That sound gives definition to words and makes them more memorable. Hence Nike, Starbucks, Exxon, Krispy Kreme, Coca-Cola. Brand names also deploy poetic metrical feet. The ones I just listed use a metrical foot called the trochee, which is a stressed syllable followed by an unstressed one: DA-da. It's the opposite of an iamb, which you may remember from studying Shakespeare's iambic pentameter in school: da-DA: "To sleep, perchance to dream." An example of an iamb used in branding is The Gap.

Trump is fond of the spondee, which is two stressed syllables (DA-DA): Fake News, Witch Hunt, Deep State. Russia Hoax is a cretic: DA-da-DA. Crooked Hillary is a bit more creative: a trochee followed by a dactyl: DA-da DA-da-da.

I can tell you from working in marketing and politics that it's scary how easy it is to manipulate how people feel and what they believe just by repeating short phrases. A lot rides on people like me choosing to be ethical. Think of the famous scene in Star *Wars: A New Hope* in which Obi-Wan Kenobi has only to say, "These aren't the droids you're looking for," and the stormtroopers let pass the droids they actually *are* looking for.[89] It's not that far from reality.

Ask yourself, for example, why so many people avoid gluten and GMOs. Face it, most do so not because of a thorough understanding of the science involved, but because the words have been made to *sound* bad, through repetition in negative contexts. The sound of "gluten" reinforces that effect: it contains echoes of "glue" and "goo." "GMO" is also potentially scary, like all acronyms are, since their meaning is obscured. When "GMO" is expanded, you discover that all three words it refers to are themselves scary-sounding: "genetically," "modified," and "organisms." None of this has anything to do with underlying facts, but it all affects beliefs and behavior. Marketers of foods containing gluten or GMOs don't waste their time arguing; they just introduce gluten-free and GMO-free brands — and stick those labels on foods that never did contain gluten or GMOs.

Tom Wolfe identified the power of a short phrase to reverse even deeply-held beliefs. Here he is in an April 8, 2008 article in *New York* magazine, analyzing a shampoo ad tag line:

> At first glance, [copywriter] Shirley Polykoff's slogan —" If I've only one life, let me live it as a blonde!" — seems like merely another example of a superficial and irritating rhetorical trope (antanaclasis) that now happens to be fashionable among advertising copywriters. But in fact the notion of "If I've only one life" challenges one of those assumptions of society that are so deep-rooted and ancient, they have no name—they are simply lived by. In this case: man's age-old belief in serial immortality...

> Most people, historically, have not lived their lives as if thinking, "I have only one life to live." Instead they have lived as if they are living their ancestors' lives and their offspring's lives and perhaps their neighbors' lives as well... For anyone to renounce the notion of serial immortality, in the West or the East, has been to defy what seems like a law of Nature.[90]

When Trump repeats brand names over and over, including *his* brand name, he's leveraging the same effect. Millions of people now do believe the mainstream news is fake, and that the name Trump represents success and power, as they believe the rest of his branded assertions.

It's like magic. Really. One reason pre-Enlightenment people believed in magic was that they had seen the power of words in their own lives. Consider the "lampoons" cast by the *filid,* the magician-poets of Dark Ages Ireland, as explained by the *Encyclopaedia Britannica*:

> They could enforce their demands by the feared lampoon (áer), or poet's curse, which not only could take away a man's reputation but, according to a widely held ancient belief, could cause physical damage or even death. Although by law a fili could be penalized for abuse of the áer, belief in its powers was strong and continued to modern times.[91]

Of course, no one believes such things now, right? Well, think of the power, even today, of a well-crafted, shame-inducing insult, whether brandished by Trump or anyone else.

Many still believe in other forms of magic as well. For example: homeopathic medicine. There isn't the slightest evidence that it works, or possibly could work. But many millions of people are convinced it does, and it has grown into a multibillion-dollar industry in the US alone. For some customers, no doubt, a homeopathic cure does help, through the placebo effect. In other words, it helps them because they believe it does.

It's magic.

Or rather, as we now know, it's psychology. Words can't summon unseen forces from a world beyond. But they can, especially through sound, rhythm, and repetition, exploit how our minds work. Repeated, catchy words and phrases capture our attention, lodge in our memory, take on a feeling of familiarity, and thereby gain our trust. None of that is magical, but it can feel like it, and work like it.

There's a great deal of research showing that it does. An essential reference is the Nobel Prize-winning psychologist Daniel Kahneman's *Thinking Fast and Slow*. The book isn't about marketing per se, but decision-making, on which marketing depends. Here's Kahneman on one of the mental mechanisms that marketers exploit, the "availability heuristic," which is often driven by emotional intensity:

> A salient event that attracts your attention will be easily retrieved from memory. Divorces among Hollywood celebrities and sex scandals among politicians attract much attention, and instances will come easily to mind. You are therefore likely to exaggerate the frequency of both Hollywood divorces and political sex scandals.
>
> A dramatic event temporarily increases the availability of its category. A plane crash that attracts media coverage will temporarily alter your feelings about the safety of flying. Accidents are on your mind, for a while, after you see a car burning at the side of the road, and the world is for a while a more dangerous place.[92]

Marketers have a simpler term for the availability heuristic: they call it the "top of mind" effect. Much of the investment in brand promotion is designed simply to make a brand "top of mind," because marketers know that we make decisions based on the information that's easiest to remember. We choose the brand that's at the top of our minds.

Another factor in the effectiveness of brand names is simple familiarity. It generates what Kahneman calls "the illusion of remembering:"

> David Stenbill, Monica Bigoutski, Shana Tirana. I just made up these names. If you encounter any of them within the next few minutes you are likely to remember where you saw them... but suppose that a few days from now you are shown a long list of names, including some minor celebrities and "new" names of people that you have never heard of; your task will be to check every name of a celebrity in the list. There is a substantial probability that you will identify David Stenbill as a well-known person...

> [Larry] Jacoby nicely stated the problem: "The experience of familiarity has a simple but powerful quality of 'pastness' that seems to indicate that it is a direct reflection of prior experience." This quality of pastness is an illusion. The truth is, as Jacoby and many followers have shown, that the name David Stenbill will look familiar when you see it because you will see it more clearly. Words that you have seen before become easier to see again...[93]

Familiarity is amplified through repetition:

> A reliable way to make people believe in falsehoods is frequent repetition, because familiarity is not easily distinguished from truth. Authoritarian institutions and marketers have always known this fact. But it was psychologists who discovered that you do not have to repeat the entire statement of a fact or idea to make it appear true. People who were repeatedly exposed to the phrase "the body temperature of a chicken" were more likely to accept as true the statement that "the body temperature of a chicken is 144°" (or any other arbitrary number). The familiarity of one phrase in the statement sufficed to make the whole statement feel familiar, and therefore true.[94]

You can test the top of mind effect, familiarity, and repetition on yourself. Try thinking of generic categories of consumer products, like detergent, cereal, sneakers, or cars. What brands come to mind most easily? Have you bought those brands?

People who have heard the phrases "Crooked Hillary," "fake news," or "deep state." over and over again, are much more likely to "buy" them, just because of the top of mind effect, familiarity, and repetition.

There are other psychological effects of the mere sounds of words, but I'll let these examples indicate how powerful those effects can be.

A similar power attaches to images. They, too, can bypass rationality and operate directly on the way our minds work. Again, there is a great deal that could be said about this, but here I'll use one more example from Kahneman, describing the effect of "priming:"

> Our vote should not be affected by the location of the polling station, for example, but it is. A study of voting patterns in precincts of Arizona in 2000 showed that the support for propositions to increase the funding of schools was significantly greater when the polling station was in a school than when it was in a nearby location. A separate experiment showed that exposing people to images of classrooms and school lockers also increased the tendency of participants to support a school initiative. The effect of the images was larger than the difference between parents and other voters![95]

It's similar with the image of Trump as a brilliant, self-made mogul. In reality, he inherited hundreds of millions of dollars and blew it. He repeatedly had to be bailed out, he paid himself handsomely from one failed business after another, and he left investors, creditors, and the IRS holding the bag.[96] But on TV, he played the role of a business genius, and millions of *Apprentice* fans were convinced that the image and the reality were the same.

The record shows this is false, but the record hardly matters. A picture really is worth a thousand words, not to mention a thousand numbers.

In 1985, English professor and cultural critic Neil Postman published *Amusing Ourselves to Death*, in which he argued that TV had changed the way we think in ways that would endanger freedom and democracy. At the time, some dismissed him as just a cranky Luddite, especially because he refused to use computers and other modern technologies. But he has been proved prescient.

Before TV, when we got most of our news in print, tyrants controlled independent thought by means of censorship, backed by the threat of violence.

George Orwell based the dystopia of 1948's *Nineteen Eighty-Four* on that form of thought control. But Postman saw that while Orwell was right about many things, he was wrong about the need for violence. On this score, Aldous Huxley had a clearer foreshadowing in 1932's *Brave New World*. Huxley predicted that people would willingly give up their freedom in return for entertainment, and by 1985, Postman could see that TV was making Huxley's vision come true:

> In the Huxleyan prophecy, Big Brother does not watch us, by his choice. We watch him, by ours. There is no need for wardens or gates or Ministries of Truth. When a population becomes distracted by trivia, when cultural life is redefined as a perpetual round of entertainments, when serious public conversation becomes a form of baby-talk, when, in short, a people become an audience and their public business a vaudeville act, then a nation finds itself at risk; culture-death is a clear possibility.

> In America, Orwell's prophecies are of small relevance, but Huxley's are well under way toward being realized. For America is engaged in the world's most ambitious experiment to accommodate itself to the technological distractions made possible by the electric plug. This is an experiment that began slowly and modestly in the mid-nineteenth century and has now, in the latter half of the twentieth, reached a perverse maturity in America's consuming love-affair with television. As nowhere else in the world, Americans have moved far and fast in bringing to a close the age of the slow-moving printed word, and have granted to television sovereignty over all of their institutions. By ushering in the Age of Television, America has given the world the clearest available glimpse of the Huxleyan future.[97]

Postman was influenced by the Canadian media theorist Marshall McLuhan, and McLuhan's insight that "the medium is the message."[98] Postman argued that in changing the way messages are delivered, technology changes the way we receive them — and eventually, the way *can* receive them. With TV, that means we stop keeping track of how one idea links to another. Instead, we simply experience one stimulating image after another, in an eternal now:

We have become so accustomed to [television's] discontinuities that we are no longer struck dumb, as any sane person would be, by a newscaster who having just reported that a nuclear war is inevitable goes on to say that he will be right back after this word from Burger King; who says, in other words, "Now... this..."[99]

Introduce the alphabet to a culture and you change its cognitive habits, its social relations, its notions of community, history and religion. Introduce the printing press with movable type, and you do the same. Introduce speed-of-light transmission of images and you make a cultural revolution. Without a vote. Without polemics. Without guerrilla resistance. Here is ideology, pure if not serene. Here is ideology without words, and all the more powerful for their absence. All that is required to make it stick is a population that devoutly believes in the inevitability of progress. And in this sense, all Americans are Marxists, for we believe nothing if not that history is moving us toward some preordained paradise and that technology is the force behind that movement.[100]

The power of words and images, independent of content and sense, goes a long way towards explaining how Trump can contradict the facts, and even himself, from day to day or moment to moment. As I write, he has made more than 20,000 false or misleading statements, while suffering no apparent loss of trust among his core supporters.[101]

Trump can command not by using force, but by putting on an ever-changing, never-ending show.

There Are Two Kinds of Truth

Nowhere are words and images more powerful than in religion. In the Abrahamic religions of Judaism, Christianity, and Islam, God's words create the world from nothing, God's words to his prophets determine the course of history, and in Christianity, God's Son is "the word made flesh."

So too, for the faithful. A credo is, literally, a statement of what "I believe," the axiom on which all other beliefs rest. A credo also defines oneself. To recite the Apostolic Creed, Shema Yisrael, or Shahada is to declare one's identity, as a Christian, a Jew, or a Muslim.

So too with any statement of faith or loyalty. Consider the Pledge of Allegiance recited by America's schoolchildren:

> I pledge allegiance to the Flag of the United States of America,
> and to the Republic for which it stands, one Nation under God,
> indivisible, with liberty and justice for all.

Within the Counter-Enlightenment worldview, a credo defines citizenship and leadership. You aren't just a United States citizen, a civic entity. You are an American, which is an ethnic identity. You don't just choose an elected official. You follow a leader in whom you believe.

This is the difference between a president and a monarch. Our Enlightenment-era Founders assumed that given the opportunity to choose, all of a monarch's subjects would prefer a democratically elected president. The Founders failed to see that for many people, gaining that freedom could feel like losing something more important: faith in a leader not just as a competent administrator but as the embodiment of the nation and of God's will. If that's what you believe your leader is, why would you want to choose another? Why would you turn away from faith, towards chaos, from confidence towards fear?

This, too, helps explain how loyalty to Trump can be so unshakeable, no matter what he says or does.

Imagine interrupting a religious service with, "But there's no evidence any of this is true!" You'd be unlikely to win many converts to your point of view. So, too, with Trump's most committed followers: they *believe* in him, and have stated that belief like a credo. Evidence challenging it isn't persuasive, it's offensive.

In contrast to a skeptic's cold doubt, such faith is often exultant: followers may believe their leader has power over reality itself: he can banish their suffering and replace it with success.

Reason, in contrast, can give you a world that probably works better. But it's also a world that can feel empty of meaning and beauty.

And empty of mystery — mystery for its own sake. Don't all of us, religious or not, seek to escape the mundane (a word derived from the Latin *mundus,* for "world), into some Narnia or Middle Earth, a place where everything doesn't *have* to make sense? We do it through novels, movies, TV shows, concerts, theme parks, video games, and our many other gateways to worlds that might still contain wonder.

We often dismiss these pursuits as "escapism." But the Danish Counter-Enlightenment philosopher Søren Kierkegaard argued that escape is crucial: life without faith is a prison.

In his *Concluding Unscientific Postscript to Philosophical Fragments* (1846), Kierkegaard compared life in a purely rational world to being trapped in an infinity of reflections. With nothing outside itself, thought thinks about thought. Escape requires a "qualitative leap" beyond reason: (often rephrased by others as a "leap of faith"). Ultimately, says Kierkegaard, "truth is subjectivity:"

> It is only when reflection comes to a halt that a beginning can
> be made, and reflection can be halted only by something else,
> and this something else is something quite other than the
> logical, because it is a decision.[102]

You must, Kierkegaard was saying, simply choose to believe. Attempting to prove the existence of God with reason was futile — and by definition, not faith.

Kierkegaard's leap from the mundane to mystery isn't the only means of escape from the prison of reason. It works the other way, too.

On the road to Damascus, Saul didn't leap towards faith. It knocked him down:

> And as he journeyed, he came near Damascus: and suddenly there shined round about him a light from heaven:
>
> And he fell to the earth, and heard a voice saying unto him, Saul, Saul, why persecutest thou me?
>
> And he said, Who art thou, Lord? And the Lord said, I am Jesus whom thou persecutest: it is hard for thee to kick against the pricks [goads].
>
> And he trembling and astonished said, Lord, what wilt thou have me to do? And the Lord said unto him, Arise, and go into the city, and it shall be told thee what thou must do.
>
> And the men which journeyed with him stood speechless, hearing a voice, but seeing no man.
>
> And Saul arose from the earth; and when his eyes were opened, he saw no man: but they led him by the hand, and brought him into Damascus.[103]

Until this moment a committed Pharisee, Saul became Paul, an apostle of Jesus.

Somewhat similarly, Gautama Siddhartha simply awakened into enlightenment, after spending years striving to achieve it. He became the Buddha.

Accounts of such revelations appear throughout history and across cultures.

I'm part of a generation of more secular seekers who thought music might be a path, with gurus like the Beatles, Jimi Hendrix, or John Coltrane leading the way. The fact that we ended up at *American Idol* and Super Bowl half-time shows doesn't necessarily mean the path wasn't there; maybe we just lost it.

Others have tried new age spirituality, meditation, drugs, sex, even sensory deprivation.

Cultural conservatism is popular in part because it promises to fulfill the same longing, the longing for something that can't be found or explained by the rational mind.

When the right argues for keeping prayer in schools, or for keeping Christmas displays in front of government buildings, the left points out that those things are in conflict with the separation of church and state.

The separation of church and state *is the problem*, says the right. On this, fundamentalists of all faiths agree: God's law should rule, not laws invented by his creatures. When Christian fundamentalists warn that America is threatened by Muslim Sharia law, to Enlightenment ears it sounds like just more paranoia: the First Amendment forbids rule by religious law. But the fear of Sharia law isn't on behalf of the First Amendment; it's on behalf of Christian religious law.

On such topics, people of the Counter-Enlightenment and the Enlightenment can talk all they want, but they won't hear each other.

That's because *they are speaking different languages* — and not only different languages, but different *kinds* of language, in which words refer to different realities.

When liberals and cultural conservatives argue over religion and other divisive cultural topics like abortion or guns, they might as well be "tap dancing about architecture," as someone once described writing about music (it's been attributed to Martin Mull, Frank Zappa, and others).

If a politician is charismatic, their rallies share characteristics with a religious service, and this is true of Trump's events. The crowd will focus its dreams and desires on him, and feel lifted up by the sense of hope coming back from the stage.

As part of my work on Barack Obama's presidential campaigns, I was at many of his rallies, and they were like that, too. To Obama's credit, he often told his staff and his supporters that the campaign wasn't about him, but about our shared goals for the country. Meanwhile, although Democrats can and do get swept up in Counter-Enlightenment transports, they land again in their Enlightenment worldview and go back to being determinedly skeptical of everything, including their own leaders, Obama among them. At their worst, they form their famous circular firing squads.

Counter-Enlightenment people feel more at home in a world of belief. If fans at a Trump rally hear him say something that isn't factually true, it's not a lie, from where they stand. It's what they *want* to be true, what *should* be true — and if you believe, what you can *make* true.

There are two kinds of truth.

To Enlightenment minds, much of what Trump says is so easily disproven, they can't imagine how his supporters don't see it.

To Counter-Enlightenment minds, Trump is speaking higher truths: statements of faith. They can't imagine how his opponents don't see that.

Ultimately, I don't believe there are two sides to misinformation: no matter how we look at reality, some things are more real than others. If you stand in the middle of the road while a bus comes speeding right at you, nothing you believe is going to make that work out any better. The reality in which COVID-19 kills people is more real than the one in which it's just a liberal hoax.

Furthermore, it's clear that when Trump lies, he isn't just exploring possibilities or being aspirational, as he sometimes claims. If someone repeatedly promotes untruths despite overwhelming evidence to the contrary, we have to conclude he's lying intentionally.

It's not surprising that Trump targets people of faith, people who have shown that they sincerely want to believe. It's the same reason snake oil sellers have always been attracted to such people, and why currently prominent ones are Trump allies, like disgraced televangelist Jim Bakker, Liberty University's Jerry Falwell, Jr., or White House religious adviser and "Prosperity Gospel" preacher Paula White. Game respects game.

But Trump's opponents are deeply mistaken if they think it will help to call his supporters dupes. That sounds a lot like mocking faith, and the faithful.

And before judging others, we should always take a look at ourselves (and maybe consider that compassion usually works better than judgment, in any case). Among the many people who are shocked at what Trump supporters believe are some who have their own irrational beliefs, like in the aforementioned homeopathy, or astrology, or numerology, or get-rich-quick schemes, or that vaccines cause autism. Irrational beliefs and behaviors are everywhere; they're just so much easier to see in other people.

By the way, if you happen to believe in one of the things I just mentioned, and maybe find my dismissal of it offensive, that feeling might be useful in imagining how anyone else feels if you tell them they're just wrong, even if all the evidence says they are.

Status & Survival

When liberals hear themselves described as enemies of America, bent on its destruction, they're often more puzzled than offended. "Where does *that* come from?" they wonder, as they look at a fellow teacher, checkout clerk, accountant, plumber, or hipster, none of them appearing to be all that threatening.

What they're missing is that a cultural threat can look like an existential threat.

Underlying the fear of losing one's culture is the fear of losing one's status within that culture. If your culture were replaced by another, you'd have no place in the new one.

The importance that human beings attach to status is often mistaken for simple vanity, but its roots are in evolution. Losing your status in a culture will cost you. Losing it in the wild can kill you. When the herd is fleeing the lions, the lowest-status individuals are at the back, where they can be picked off.

Research shows that among humans, loss of status can cause misery, anger, and even self-defeating behavior. Psychologist Adam Waytz summarized it in an article for *Scientific American:*

> Ongoing efforts to maintain a positive view of oneself despite economic and social hardships can engage psychological defense mechanisms that are ultimately self-defeating. Instead of ingratiating themselves to those around them – this is the successful strategy for status attainment — low-status individuals may be more prone to bullying and hostile behavior, especially when provoked. Research identifying factors that lead to successful status-seeking provides some optimism, though. Individuals capable of signaling their worth to others rather than being preoccupied with signaling their

worth to themselves may be able to break the self-defeating
cycle of low-status behavior.[104]

When Trump claims that before he came along, America was being exploited
and mocked, it sounds ridiculous to those who have felt safe in the modern,
globalized world. The USA is the richest, most powerful country in history. *Of
course* we weren't being exploited and mocked.

But that's not how it looked to Trump's base, who did feel exploited and
mocked. And since they tend to see their nationality as the same as their ethnicity,
their nation was being exploited and mocked.

Under Trump, they feel like they're great, if only because he keeps telling
them so.

Meanwhile Trump's opponents keep telling them how un-great they are.
Trump's former chief adviser Steve Bannon welcomed that: "Let them call you
racists... Wear it as a badge of honor," he said, knowing how it could strengthen
support for Trump.[105]

Hillary Clinton, who exemplifies Enlightenment rationality to a politically
fatal fault, made Bannon's point for him, with her now-legendary "deplorables"
comment.[106] As an insult, that term probably felt worse than "racists," because at
least "racists" might be leveled at social equals. "Deplorables" is so fancy; so
high-handed; so better-than-you.

Hillary's defense for her comment was that some Trump supporters — for
example, the KKK members and the Nazis — really *are* deplorable, which they
are. Hillary said that she regretted saying that as many as "half" of Trump fans
were deplorables; the actual ratio was probably lower.

Oh, well, that makes it all fine.

No, it doesn't. Trump's base wasn't insulted over a percentage, they were
insulted over their identity.

Identity, as we've seen, is a big reason for their fierce loyalty to Trump. He
defends them, talks like them, and acts like them — or at least how they might
act if they too could live the role of a billionaire. Looking at him, they feel like
he *is* them.

Contrast the awkward simulation of a "regular American guy" that was John
Kerry posing in brand new hunting togs, or Hillary Clinton hoisting a beer in a
bar.

It's not that liberals just can't get it. Franklin Delano Roosevelt never did a thing to hide his blueblood background. But working people loved FDR. That was because he spoke with them personally and emotionally — including through the skillful use of the media in his friendly, empathetic, and encouraging fireside chats.

On the 2020 presidential campaign trail, Sen. Amy Klobuchar often told a powerful story about FDR:

> After he died, his body was transported by train through America. At one station, a reporter asked a man who was in tears if he knew President Roosevelt. And the grieving man said, "No, I didn't know President Roosevelt. But he knew me."[107]

Because Trump knows how to create a similar, if more fear-driven, sense of identification with his people, an attack on him becomes an attack on them. So it simply doesn't matter how well the attack is supported by facts and logic. Facts and logic may just make it worse.

Meritocracy & Corruption:
How Wrong Can Look Right

L ooking at the importance of status leads us to another Enlightenment blind spot: the cruelty of meritocracy. To most Enlightenment egalitarians, meritocracy appears self-evidently good: surely, people should succeed based on their skills and accomplishments, not on hereditary privilege or, worse, corruption.

But consider the worldview in which that seems self-evident: it's the one inhabited by meritocracy's winners.

And how did they get where they are? If you happened to be born smart, you didn't choose that, you won a genetic lottery. If you happened to be born into a stable, solvent family that provided you with a good education and useful social connections, that was luck, too.

Meanwhile some people, through no fault of their own, are born with about average intelligence, or less. Or they may be born into conditions that make it less likely that they wind up well-educated, or emotionally healthy and resilient.

Pluck and hard work matter, of course, but even so, a meritocracy has a lot in common with a hereditary aristocracy. And in fact, that's how meritocracy has played out, ever since British sociologist Michael Young first warned us about it in *The Rise of the Meritocracy* (1958), only to see his warning ignored. Instead, meritocracy was widely adopted as a model.[108] Young's critical analysis has since been expanded upon by, among others, Chris Hayes in *Twilight of the Elites: America After Meritocracy* (2013) and Daniel Markovits in *The Meritocracy Trap: How America's Foundational Myth Feeds Inequality, Dismantles the Middle Class, and Devours the Elite* (2019).

In one sense, meritocracy is even worse than aristocracy. Under an aristocracy, at least the "lower orders" have the comfort of knowing their lives could never have worked out otherwise. Like everyone else, they were born into the class in which they would die. But meritocracy entails the assumption that you make your own fate: if you end up in a low-status job, it's because of your lack of merit.

Thus, people making their way through life at an average-or-below level of status may constantly feel judged and humiliated by those with higher status, even when it looks as if they're only imagining it. Everywhere they turn, the system itself judges and humiliates them.

In light of the luck and even unfairness upon which meritocracy rests, the appeal of populist tribalism becomes a lot easier to see. If you were born unlucky, meritocracy is not a path to opportunity, but to loss. Your tribe becomes your defense: life doesn't have your back, but your tribe does.

This is another reason why pointing out all the ways Trump is a failure can be a losing tactic. Since he has identified himself so strongly with his base, you're calling them failures, too.

It also explains how to his supporters, Trump's corruption may not look like much of a problem. If you believe the system will never allow people like you to win, corruption can become not only normalized, but expected.

This is what is observed in societies with weak institutions: tribal loyalty is valued much more highly than obedience to a set of rules in which no one really believes. It's a frequent obstacle to overcoming corruption in the delivery of foreign aid, as was found by researchers at Tufts University's Fletcher School of Law and Diplomacy:

> In certain specific circumstances, social norms can be more influential than personal attitudes, knowledge, or morals in orienting people's choices. These social expectations and the prospect of social reward or punishment often lead people to engage in practices they personally do not agree with…
>
> The [Ugandan] police officer, judge, or magistrate who demands bribes may do so in part because lack of enforcement of anti-corruption laws makes it easy for him to get away with it. But he is also experiencing significant pressure from family

and friends to accumulate wealth and to provide for them once
he has reached this important position. Thus, even if he wants
to act with integrity, if he does not accumulate sufficient
wealth, he will be criticized, ostracized, and potentially
punished by his family in other ways.[109]

Donald Trump came up in the notoriously corrupt New York real estate
business, in which working with crooks, such as Mafia-backed contractors, was
not unusual.[110] As loss of faith in American institutions has spread, the cultural
norms that shaped Trump in New York have come to match the expectations of
many people across the country.

The Evolution of Tribalism

I n a world of corruption, tribalism can make sense as a situational response. But tribalism is also wired into us. Evolution selects for it, as Charles Darwin described in *The Descent of Man* (1871):

> When two tribes of primeval man, living in the same country, came into competition, if (other circumstances being equal) the one tribe included a great number of courageous, sympathetic and faithful members, who were always ready to warn each other of danger, to aid and defend each other, this tribe would succeed better and conquer the other... The advantage which disciplined soldiers have over undisciplined hordes follows chiefly from the confidence which each man feels in his comrades... Selfish and contentious people will not cohere, and without coherence nothing can be effected. A tribe rich in the above qualities would spread and be victorious over other tribes, but in the course of time it would, judging from all past history, be in its turn overcome by some other tribe still more highly endowed. Thus the social and moral qualities would tend slowly to advance and be diffused throughout the world.[111]

Embedded in the evolutionary explanation is competition over limited resources. This is important in understanding how it is that racism is not innate — children have to be taught to be racists — but tribalism is. Differences among people don't carry any value one way or the other, until tribes form and have to compete over resources. *Then* the stuff gets real.

Realistic Conflict Theory is based on the primacy of competition in spurring tribal conflict. It was illustrated by the Robbers Cave Experiment of 1954, which was conducted on two arbitrarily-assembled groups of summer campers. Here are some of the results recorded by the experiment's designers, Muzafer Sherif and Carolyn W. Sherif:

> When the two groups, whose members were not unfriendly initially, came together in a series of activities where one could achieve its goal only at the expense of the other group, in time, **the rivalry changed to open conflict between them.**
>
> Members of each group developed hostile and unfriendly attitudes toward the other group and its members. When asked to rate the members of the other groups on several traits (such as "brave," "sneaky," "cheats"), **the boys in each group gave extremely negative ratings** ("all of them are cheats"), indicating the rudiments of intergroup stereotypes.
>
> By the end of the period, **social distance had developed between the two groups,** such that neither wanted to have anything to do with the other, nor to be in any activities at the same time and place.
>
> ...There were changes in the status structure of several groups in these experiments. For example, the leader of one had been very skillful at coordinating activities before, but shrank from intergroup encounters... and avoided physical conflict. He was rapidly replaced by another boy who rallied the group. In another group, **a large boy who had been "put in his place" because he roughed up smaller boys, became a hero in intergroup conflict** for his prowess in raids and scuffles.
>
> Each group had new norms added to their repertory. These norms largely pertained to treatment of the other group, forbidding expression of kind thoughts about the other, ruling out contact between them, and regulating how one should behave in their presence.[112] (Emphasis added.)

Inter-group conflict in response to competition: this is what has happened in American society at large since the sixties. As I noted earlier, the initially broad support for civil rights fell after measures such as integration and school busing were introduced. Some of the white Americans who previously felt more or less friendly towards minorities now perceived threats to their interests.

The sense of grievance felt by many whites has only grown since, as diversity and immigration have increased while wages have remained flat. Visible differences became the basis of intergroup conflict, even though those differences were only tangentially related to competition for resources. Martin Luther King, Jr. evangelized for a future in which Americans were judged only by "the content of their character," but since his assassination, identity politics has gained currency among whites and among minorities.

A demagogue like Trump, posing as the strongman who can solve the problems of "real Americans" was well-positioned to profit.

Both evolution and tribalism may in turn be the sources of our moral judgments, including our propensity to make very divisive ones.

The social psychologist Jonathan Haidt explains the evolutionary roots of moralism, and how it divides us, in *The Righteous Mind* (2013):

> An obsession with righteousness (leading inevitably to self-righteousness) is the normal human condition. It is a feature of our evolutionary design, not a bug or error that crept into minds that would otherwise be objective and rational. Our righteous minds made it possible for human beings—but no other animals—to produce large cooperative groups, tribes, and nations without the glue of kinship. But at the same time, our righteous minds guarantee that our cooperative groups will always be cursed by moralistic strife. Some degree of conflict among groups may even be necessary for the health and development of any society…
>
> People bind themselves into political teams that share moral narratives. Once they accept a particular narrative, they become blind to alternative moral worlds.[113]

Psychologist and complexity theorist Mirta Galesic grew up in the former Yugoslavia, and watched tribalism tear her country apart. Following the death of the dictator Tito, formerly suppressed ethnic divisions resurfaced, and people who had lived together peaceably for years began attacking each other. Witnessing the violence spawned Galesic's intense interest in group behavior, which she now studies from bases at the Santa Fe Institute and Berlin's Max

Planck Institute. She told me about it in an interview for my podcast, *Dastardly Cleverness in the Service of Good:*

> When I was 16 or so the country started to fall apart... It was a transforming period of my life, when I saw how a seemingly stable system suddenly collapses... in a very short period of time. And I noticed how people, although they have access to all the information about different points of view, choose to pay attention to one particular point of view that supports their group... Since then, I recognized that there is no simple model that could explain human behavior and human reasoning, but it must be some interaction between cognition and social environment that makes us behave in what we think are irrational ways.[114]

In 2018, Galesic and partners published research indicating that how people vote can be predicted in part by how they think their group will vote:

> Election outcomes can be difficult to predict. A recent example is the 2016 US presidential election, in which Hillary Clinton lost five states that had been predicted to go for her, and with them the White House. Most election polls ask people about their own voting intentions: whether they will vote and, if so, for which candidate. We show that, compared with own-intention questions, social-circle questions that ask participants about the voting intentions of their social contacts improved predictions of voting in the 2016 US and 2017 French presidential elections. Responses to social-circle questions predicted election outcomes on national, state and individual levels, helped to explain last-minute changes in people's voting intentions and provided information about the dynamics of echo chambers among supporters of different candidates.[115]

It's not just that it was Trump who came down the golden escalator in the summer of 2015. Once the tribe has spoken, anyone might command loyalty.

The Culture of Tribalism:
Blood, Soil & Loyalty

F ollowing the Enlightenment, tribalism was seen as a vestige of the pre-modern world that would inevitably wither away. The opposite happened. As modern society became ever more rationally civic, ethnic tribalism resurged. It now saturates our popular culture.

You may have noticed an echo from the hugely successful TV show *Survivor* at the end of the last chapter: "The tribe has spoken."[116] *Survivor's* creator, Mark Burnett, was also behind the show that probably did more than anything else to fashion Trump's image as a strong leader: *The Apprentice*. On both shows, the drama is based in tribalism and tribal leadership.

Tribalism, often in stereotypical form, has influenced culture for centuries. In the Age of Reason, global explorers brought back artifacts of exotic foreign cultures, which excited fascination at home. From there the timeline goes through the Enlightenment, with Rousseau and his "noble savages;" the Romantic Era's fascination with Arabia and the East; the art of the American West; the works of Kipling and other expatriates of the British Empire; the paintings and sculptures of the Fauves, Gaugin, and Picasso; Stravinsky's *Rite of Spring;* jazz and other forms of "ethnic" music; sixties counterculture; charismatic religions and cults; punk; electronic dance music (EDM); the "modern tribalism" trend, which has added tattoos and piercings to the standard fashion palette; and the aforementioned rise of identity politics, which pairs ethnic nationalism, often uneasily, with civic nationalism.

Max Weber saw that in modern times, the influence of tribalism would grow all the greater. Weber may not have predicted Coachella, but he did grasp the cultural effects of rationalization and depersonalization on modern society.

Earlier, I quoted from his lecture "Science as a Vocation," on the topic of disenchantment. Later in that same passage, he turns his gaze to the future, and predicts that rationalist, alienated moderns would try to re-enchant the world by inventing new arts, religions, and fanatical theories:

> ...It is no accident that our greatest art is intimate rather than monumental. Nor is it a matter of chance that today it is only in the smallest groups, between individual human beings, pianissimo, that you find the pulsing beat that in bygone days heralded the prophetic spirit that swept through great communities like a firestorm and welded them together. If we attempt artificially to "invent" a sense of monumental art, this leads only to wretched monstrosities of the kind we have seen in the many artistic works of the last twenty years. If we attempt to construct new religious movements without a new, authentic prophecy, this only gives rise to something equally monstrous in terms of inner experience, which can only have an even more dire effect. And academic prophecies can only ever produce fanatical sects, but never a genuine community.[117]

We don't need to agree that all such developments produce cultural "monstrosities" to acknowledge that, back in 1917, Weber foresaw the trends that have dominated popular art, religion, and philosophy ever since.

Weber is also a guide to the rise of charismatic leaders. In his 1919 lecture "Politics as a Vocation," he identified three possible foundations of legitimate authority:

> First, the authority of "the eternal past," of **custom,** sanctified by a validity that extends back into the mists of time and is perpetuated by habit. This is "traditional" rule, as exercised by patriarchs and patrimonial rulers of the old style. Second, there is the authority of the extraordinary, personal gift of grace or **charisma,** that is, the wholly personal devotion to, and a personal trust in, the revelations, heroism, or other leadership qualities of an individual. This is "charismatic" rule of the kind practiced by prophets or—in the political sphere—the elected warlord or the ruler chosen by popular vote, the great demagogue, and the leaders of political parties. Lastly, there is rule by virtue of **"legality,"** by virtue of the belief in the

> validity of legal statutes and practical "competence" based on
> rational rules. This type of rule is based on a person's
> willingness to carry out statutory duties obediently. Rule of this
> kind is to be found in the modern "servant of the state" and all
> those agents of power who resemble him in this respect.[118]
> (Emphasis added.)

The 2016 contest between Donald Trump and Hillary Clinton pitted a charismatic demagogue against a legalistic civil servant. That is the essence of Counter-Enlightenment vs. Enlightenment leadership. Trump's hostile relationship with German Prime Minister Angela Merkel is a similar opposition.

While Trump's rise to power was based on charisma, it had little to do with Weber's first source of authority, tradition. Before he was elected, Trump had shown little interest in that.

But it's different now that he's *in* power and ruling in many ways like a monarch — even toying with the idea of never leaving office, unless perhaps to hand the crown to Ivanka or Don Junior.[119]

Evolution explains how tribalism may be in our genes. Culture shows how, metaphorically, and sometimes literally, it's in our blood.

Think of how character was determined throughout pre-Enlightenment history. Every person was assumed to have an essential nature, which was identified with their blood. Blood could be either noble or base, or some mixture of the two.

The blood of the monarch carried the noblest attributes of the entire nation. This is the deeper meaning of Louis XIV's (possibly apocryphal) *"L'etat c'est moi"* — "The state is me." It also means "I am the state."

The land, too, was believed to have an essential nature. It was the native soil, the homeland, the motherland, or the fatherland.[120] All of these names implied that the people inherited their natures from the land: blood from soil.

To swear fealty to a person who embodied the homeland — whose blood was one with the soil — was to create a bond that was unbreakable unto and even beyond death.

This is why we still speak of blood oaths, and why ceremonies of faith and allegiance so often involve figurative or literal blood — and in the case of the

Catholic Eucharist, a transfiguration from one to the other. We confront and transcend death itself in ritual — or in reality, in the most violent rites.

Given what Trump has been able to get away with so far, we have to assume that if he did shoot someone in the middle of Fifth Avenue, some of his followers would believe it was justified. Any justification needed is already contained within his person, as the symbolic monarch.

Attorney General William Barr is not far from making the legal case for that, as he acts on his belief in the theory of the unitary executive, which claims that Article II of the Constitution gives the president enormous power. One of Trump's impeachment attorneys went all the way there, asserting to Congress that any prosecution for a shooting would have to wait until Trump left office.[121] Trump himself has said the president's "authority is total,"[122] that he can do "whatever I want."[123]

Far from needing to be excused, the commission of violent acts by monarchs has often *enhanced* their authority. This is why executions were so often carried out in public. Simply killing someone would not be enough. An execution was theater written in blood.

Trump stages symbolic executions, by inciting rallygoers against protesters or the press, or in devising elaborately humiliating ways to fire people. He's often accused of being a sadist, but, true or not, that doesn't capture the authority-building utility of such behavior.

I'm not suggesting that Trump really might shoot someone. But the fact that we have to wonder what would happen next shows the power that a tribal leader can command, once he was won total personal loyalty, as the personification of the nation.

In the face of such power, what chance does reason have?

Identity Politics

S o far, I've talked about identity mostly as it appears within the Counter-Enlightenment worldview, in the form of tribal identity. But identity is behind political behavior in both of the two nations, and is a source of conflict between them and within them.

I sometimes summarize politics with three I's: Ideas, Interests, and Identity. People who haven't worked in the field, especially those of the pro-science, Enlightenment bent, often wonder why politics can't just focus on the first I: get the right Idea, and act on it —Socrates asked the same question, and answered it with his advocacy for the philosopher king. Interests and Identity explain why that won't work in real life.

Interests will lead people to reject a good idea for what serves them better personally. They may very well convince themselves they're just doing what's right: "It is difficult to get a man to understand something, when his salary depends upon his not understanding it," as Upton Sinclair said. So did William Jennings Bryan before him, in different words: "It is useless to argue with a man whose opinion is based upon a personal or pecuniary interest; the only way to deal with him is to outvote him."[124]

Identity will also override the dispassionate discussion of ideas, either because an idea might threaten the interests of one's identity group, or because it might threaten the identity itself. Removing Christmas displays from government property may look like the right idea, given our separation of church and state, and it hardly harms anyone's interests, but some Christians oppose it as a matter of identity. So it is with many other political decisions that intersect with identity, whether religious or cultural.

Although "identity politics" seems new, it has always existed in one form or another. White Anglo-Saxon Protestants have always practiced it, although often unconsciously. WASP was the traditional, default American identity, and WASPs were the beneficiaries of what in effect was a permanent affirmative action program, though it was largely unrecognized. It's hard to see the sea you swim in. No doubt for that reason, the Founders, who were strong on Ideas and Interests, underestimated the power of Identity when they were designing our Constitutional democracy.

More recently, identity politics has been understood as the version practiced by minorities. It tends to be much more noticeable, because it disrupts what until recently was normality.

The dialogue about identity politics is concomitantly confused: Necessary? Evil? Necessary evil?

When bigoted white people practice identity politics, it's easy to deplore, because white people are the traditionally dominant identity group. And if a Martin Luther King, Jr. or a Cesar Chavez practices identity politics, it's easy to celebrate them bravely standing up for the oppressed.

But in less clear-cut cases, the conversation quickly gets complicated — the more so when we try to think about it within an Enlightenment framework, since *not* thinking can make things so much simpler.

For example, WASPs who have grown up in the Enlightenment tradition are comfortable critiquing their own culture, but because that critique leads them to be wary of prejudice against other cultures, they may become anxiously tongue-tied and end up excusing behavior in another culture that they wouldn't stand for in their own. We see it, for example, in the excuses some liberals make for Louis Farrakhan's anti-Semitism. This strikes me as a form of paternalism on their part. Ironically enough, it shares characteristics with old colonialist belief in the White Man's Burden. "*We* can stand up to a critique of our culture, but these others are more child-like, and need to be protected from such concerns."

Another example: Among my fellow liberals, a form of piety about women and minorities has emerged, which leads to assigning essentialist qualities to identity *if* those qualities are positive, but denying that such differences are even possible if they might be negative. So, for example, we can assert that women are naturally better at intuition, multi-tasking, or cooperation, but we would never say that women have any natural deficits. Furthermore, it's contextual. So we'll link positive qualities to female biological sex much of the time, but in the context of gender politics, we may have to deny that sex confers *any* essential qualities, because gender is supposed to be socially constructed — unless it isn't, say because we're among the subset of feminists who exclude trans women from their ranks.

It strikes me that both the positive and negative forms of essentialism are based on group stereotypes, which unavoidably exclude individuals. That's true whether we're claiming that "all women are intuitive" or that "all women are bad at math," or that "a woman is whoever identifies as a woman," or "not around here, she isn't." But of course there are plenty of women who are not particularly intuitive, and plenty who are brilliant at math, and sex and gender turn out to be complicated. There are all kinds of people in the world — as many kinds as there are people, I would argue.

Whatever essential differences might be present in any person or group, they're either there or not, independent of whatever cultural interpretation we want to attach to them. Surely, people are equal because they're people, not because they're special.

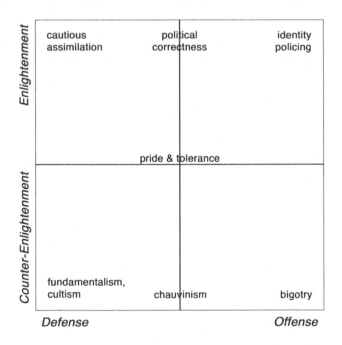

My view is that talking about identity politics is easier and more productive if we can think about it in more than one dimension. Picture a graph defined by two axes: let the X-axis run from Defense to Offense and the Y-axis run from the Counter-Enlightenment to the Enlightenment.

At the upper left, we have people who are aware of their rights within the Enlightenment worldview, but who are trying to stay safe by neither asserting themselves nor overtly expressing their identity. Examples might be closeted gays, or those pre-Civil Rights Era African Americans who didn't want to "rock the boat."

At the lower left are people who reject the modern, Enlightenment-based world and isolate themselves from it, perhaps in a cult.

At the lower right, unthinking ethnocentrism combines with aggression to produce racism or religious intolerance.

At the upper right is rationalistic "discourse" about identity, combined with enforcement of the currently acceptable definition.

In a pluralistic society, we obviously don't want what's at the lower right: unthinking, aggressive bigotry. Neither do we want the defensive crouch at the upper left, nor the retreat into a monoculture at the lower left. And the alternative doesn't have to be the upper right: political correctness or identity policing.

An amazing variety of cultural expressions is a big part of what makes America great. It's not just diversity: *American culture wouldn't exist* without the interplay of many cultures, from the British Isles, Europe, Africa, the Jewish diaspora, Latin America, Asia, Polynesia, and everywhere else, as well as from every religion and every gender identity. Think of our movies, music, and even our sense of humor, and then try to imagine any of them without the influences of multiple cultures.

How do we protect that legacy?

As the practice of identity politics moves along the X-axis away from Defense, we at first gain the shared benefits of free, equal people expressing their different cultures. But as that progress tips from pride to aggression — "My group is not just equal to, but better than other groups" — then identity politics becomes less and less compatible with civic nationalism.

As with defending identity, so with defining it.

At the Counter-Enlightenment end of the scale, we're immersed in culture, which can bestow a sense of security and connection. But it can also mean we're not thinking, which can make way for rigidity and intolerance. This is the domain of cultural chauvinism. Moving along the axis towards the Enlightenment introduces awareness and reflection. As with the Defense/Offense axis, to a point this is a good thing. It's through awareness and reflection that America and other Enlightenment-based countries have made progress towards fulfilling the foundational promise of equality.

But as identity politics moves farther along the axis towards Enlightenment thinking, it can go too far into the head and away from the heart: cultural identity becomes intellectualized. What makes a culture rich is not rational: faith, symbolism, art, cuisine, clothing, traditions. When we're all the way into our heads, we get identity as a political construct, often one that's decreed from above.

This is what seems to have happened with the Latinx identity. If you're thinking in the Enlightenment mode, of course we should try to free our thinking of gender bias. So, looking at a Romance language like Spanish, which has gender built into it, why not remove gender from references to people? Makes sense.

Except that whoever decided this forgot to consult members of the culture they wanted to change. In a survey conducted by the polling firm ThinkNow, only two percent of Latinos liked the idea of being called Latinx, as the firm's Mario Carrasco described in a post on Medium:

> While my colleagues and I are progressive on social issues, as researchers, we have to put aside our personal biases and render advice based on the best available empirical evidence. To examine the acceptance of "Latinx" our firm conducted a nationwide poll of Latinos using a 508-person sample that is demographically representative of Census figures, yielding a ± 5% margin of error with a 95% confidence interval.

> We presented our respondents with seven of the most common terms used to describe Latinos and asked them to select the one that best describes them. When it came to "Latinx," there was near unanimity. Despite its usage by academics and cultural influencers, 98% of Latinos prefer other terms to describe their

ethnicity. Only 2% of our respondents said the label accurately describes them, making it the least popular ethnic label among Latinos.[125]

It turns out that a culture may resist definition by committee. Columbia University linguistics professor John McWhorter wrote an article for *The Atlantic* about why "Latinx" has failed to catch on beyond a small group of "intellectuals, journalists, and university officials," while "African American" did become popular:

> The reason for the difference is familiar to linguists who study how languages change. Although it may seem that new elements of a language settle in when regular people imitate famous or prestigious people, more generally, new language comes from below. That is, tomorrow's words and constructions are ones that even today feel not swanky but ordinary, like "us." One used to say that a house "was building." Being built began as a neologism associated with people of lesser education, but was eventually adopted by everyone else.[126]

The pejorative use of "politically correct" is often a cheap way of escaping accountability for bigotry, which isn't "politically incorrect," but morally wrong. It's not "playing the race card" to object to racism. But there is a form of political correctness that even many non-bigots find intolerant and undemocratic. The problem with it is contained in the term itself (when used unironically): how can politics, which is not just about ideas, but interests and identity as well, ever be "correct?"

Political correctness is what we find at the far end of the Counter-Enlightenment/Enlightenment axis, and moving rightward towards Offense. It's what we see in the seemingly endless litigation of identity that happens in some neighborhoods of Twitter, or in the intolerance on some college campuses, where faculty members anxiously strive to show how woke they are, and visiting speakers with unpopular opinions can be barred or even threatened, at which point we're all the way into identity policing.

This kind of identity politics appears to be descended from Scholastic philosophy, which reduced the mysteries of faith to the parsing of doctrine, and from Puritanism, which defined and enforced rigid cultural norms. It shares that heritage with even worse forms of intolerance and thought control, which I think we can all take as a warning.

With identity politics, we can borrow the advice offered by both the ancient Greek poet Hesiod and the Buddha: Follow the middle way.

The Problem of Evil: When Cruelty Is the Point

S ometimes, as Adam Serwer wrote in the October, 2018 issue of *The Atlantic*, "The Cruelty Is the Point." He described the glee on the faces of people photographed at a lynching some decades ago:

> These grinning men were someone's brother, son, husband, father. They were human beings, people who took immense pleasure in the utter cruelty of torturing others to death—and were so proud of doing so that they posed for photographs with their handiwork, jostling to ensure they caught the eye of the lens, so that the world would know they'd been there. Their cruelty made them feel good, it made them feel proud, it made them feel happy. And it made them feel closer to one another.[127]

Serwer's article attributed the same feelings to Trump supporters. I don't believe cruelty is the point for all or even most of them, but it looks like it is for some, such as those who cheer at the mockery of sexual assault victims or disabled people, or at the sight of immigrant children in cages.

There is danger in this kind of observation, though, as there is with any moral judgment: We attribute evil to other people without recognizing where it comes from, or how it may be present in all of us in one form or another. However tempting it may be to judge Trump and his supporters, or others, it does not solve the problem of evil, and in fact is more likely to perpetuate it. Our legacy of violence is a legacy of seeing evil in others and trying to destroy it.

As history makes all too clear, cruelty can be summoned even from peaceful, law-abiding people. Whenever torture or executions have been staged in public, they have always drawn a crowd.

The tension between impulse and control — *Civilization and Its Discontents,* in Freud's phrase — is ever-present in our cultural history. Impulse may take the happy form of a drunken reveler, like Dionysus, shucking off the rules his brother Apollo wants to follow so strictly. But sometimes, the revels devolve into chaos, when all bonds of civilization are cut, and humanity's worst instincts are set free to exult in harm for its own sake.

The Emperor Nero lived in such a state. He once recruited his fellow Romans to join him there for a night. Historian Tom Holland describes it in his book, *Dominion: How the Christian Revolution Remade the World* (2019):

> Such it was to live as a hero of myth. What, in a city ruled by a superhuman figure, were mere proprieties? Rome itself was rendered complicit in their repeated and spectacular subversion. In the summer of AD 64, a great street party was thrown to celebrate the new order of things. In the very heart of the city, a lake was filled with sea-monsters. Along its edge, brothels were staffed with whores ranging from the cheapest streetwalkers to the most blue-blooded of aristocrats. For a single night, to the delight of the men who visited them and knew that the women were forbidden to refuse anyone, there was no slave or free. 'Now a minion would take his mistress in the presence of his master; now a gladiator would take a girl of noble family before the gaze of her father.'[128]

Throughout the long history of rape, torture, pillage, and humiliation, the dark bacchanal beckons.

Why?

Freud wrote of the death drive, sometimes called Thanatos, an instinctive urge to destroy, which struggles for control with Eros, the life-force.

The battle has deep cultural roots. Before Yahweh and Satan appeared in the Hebrew scriptures, the Babylonian *Enuma Elish* told how the young god Marduk, sometimes called Bel, killed the giant dragon Tiamat and created humanity from her corpse:

He let fly an arrow and pierced her belly,
He tore open her entrails and slit her inwards,
He bound her and extinguished her life,
He threw down her corpse and stood on it.[129]

In the Bible, God creates Adam and Eve, who live in paradise until they succumb to temptation by the serpent and eat of the Tree of Knowledge. Thus is established the Judeo-Christian tradition of humanity's sinful nature, requiring God's guidance and redemption.

The Enlightenment overthrew that tradition, replacing original sin with the concept of natural rights, and Rousseau's belief in people's innate goodness.

But Counter-Enlightenment thinkers held to the vision of a fallen world. Rousseau didn't speak for them. Rather it was Thomas Hobbes, who described the state of humanity in nature as "the war of all against all."[130]

To this day, one way of understanding the difference between the descendants of the Enlightenment and the Counter-Enlightenment, including the cultural left and right, is to think of them as the descendants of either Rousseau or Hobbes.

Those who believe in Rousseauian innocence hold that children only go astray if they are failed by their families or society.

Others still believe in evil, either as a religious precept, or in an even more terrifying secular form: meaningless, empty horror, such as Kurtz confronts in Joseph Conrad's *Heart of Darkness*. I have more to say on this in the next chapter.

The broad consensus among contemporary psychologists is that all of us have the potential to do good or harm, depending on how we were born and how we grew up: it's nature *and* nurture. Research indicates that some children are genetically predisposed to behavioral problems, but for all children, upbringing is highly predictive of what comes later, including substance abuse, crime, and early death.[131] Children who used to be seen as "just bad" — the ones who apparently lack a conscience or who even take pleasure in hurting others — often turn out, heartbreakingly, to have suffered neglect or abuse in infancy.

While science may not solve the problem of evil at its origins — Why does it exist at all? — it might explain why generation after generation, there is a reservoir of cruelty waiting to be tapped.

It's striking how many people tell stories from childhood that they see as having forged their character, but which also sound like abuse. Roger Ailes used to relate how his father once invited him to jump from a bunk bed into his arms, only to let young Roger crash to the floor. The point was to teach him never to trust anyone — it certainly would have taught him not to trust his father, which must have left quite an emotional scar. This story is surprisingly common. I know people who tell it.

In her book *Too Much and Never Enough,* Donald Trump's niece Mary Trump, a clinical psychologist, describes emotional neglect and abuse suffered by her uncle, starting when he was just two and a half years old. Illness suddenly rendered his mother, also named Mary, absent much of the time. Young Donald and his siblings were left in the care of their father Fred, whom author Mary Trump says was a "sociopath:"

> The greater their distress… the more Fred rebuffed them. He did not like to have demands made of him, and the annoyance provoked by his children's neediness set up a dangerous tension in the Trump household: by engaging in behaviors that were biologically designed to trigger soothing, comforting responses from their parents, the little boys instead provoked their father's anger or indifference when they were most vulnerable. For Donald and Robert, "needing" became equated with humiliation, despair, and hopelessness…

> In order to cope, Donald began to develop powerful but primitive defenses, marked by an increasing hostility to others and a seeming indifference to his mother's absence and father's neglect… In place of [having his emotional needs met] grew a kind of grievance and behaviors—including bullying, disrespect, and aggressiveness—that served their purpose in the moment but became more problematic over time… Once Fred started paying attention to his loud and difficult second son, he came to value them. Put another way, Fred Trump came to validate, encourage, and champion the things about Donald that rendered him essentially unlovable and that were in part the direct result of Fred's abuse.[132]

Paul Schwartzman and Michael E. Miller's book *Trump Revealed* (2016) contains this story about young Donald's behavior:

Dennis Burnham was four years younger and lived around the corner from Donald. He inherited his own impression of his neighbor from his mother, who warned that he should "stay away from the Trumps."

"Donald was known to be a bully, I was a little kid, and my parents didn't want me beaten up," said Burnham, 65, a business consultant in Texas.

Once when she left Dennis in a playpen in a back yard adjoining the Trumps' property, Martha Burnham returned to find Donald throwing rocks at her son. "She saw Donald standing at the fence," Dennis Burnham said, "using the playpen for target-practice."[133]

Given the adult Trump's seeming delight in tormenting people, while constantly seeking adulation for himself, one might well ask, "Was he just born without a conscience?"

Unlikely.

Like everyone else, Trump was probably born with about as much potential to be compassionate as to be cruel.

Someday, if he can, the President would do society a service by telling us more about his childhood. It may end up explaining a lot about recent history.

Beyond Evil: The Hollow Men

The discussion in the previous chapter locates evil within individual human hearts, as formed by our individual histories. But as I suggested with my reference to Kurtz in Conrad's *Heart of Darkness*, there's a bleaker view. It emerges from inhuman systems that make the individual psyche irrelevant.

In *Heart of Darkness,* that system is European imperialism, ravaging the Belgian Congo in the pursuit of profits. Kurtz had started his career as an idealist, deluding himself, as had the rest of Europe, that he was bringing the light of civilization to backward savages. But as he traveled deeper into the "dark continent," acquiring ever more ivory at the cost of ever more African lives, he discovered that the heart of darkness was the void within himself:

> ...There was something wanting in him—some small matter which, when the pressing need arose, could not be found under his magnificent eloquence. Whether he knew of this deficiency himself I can't say. I think the knowledge came to him at last— only at the very last. But the wilderness had found him out early, and had taken on him a terrible vengeance for the fantastic invasion. I think it had whispered to him things about himself which he did not know, things of which he had no conception till he took counsel with this great solitude—and the whisper had proved irresistibly fascinating. It echoed loudly within him because he was hollow at the core....

T.S. Eliot quoted *Heart of Darkness* as the introduction to his poem "The Hollow Men:"

"Mistah Kurtz, he dead."

We are the hollow men
We are the stuffed men
Leaning together
Headpiece filled with straw. Alas!
Our dried voices, when
We whisper together
Are quiet and meaningless
As wind in dry grass
Or rats' feet over broken glass
In our dry cellar...

One of Conrad's many intellectual descendants was his fellow Pole Czeslaw Milosz, whose poem "Child of Europe" I quoted from earlier. Milosz lived under Nazi and then Soviet domination, before defecting and moving to the United States. Americans, he wrote, are as naïve as children. Unlike citizens of old, suffering Europe, we have been spared the full, awful knowledge of what individuals might do once they have surrendered to an inhuman system.

In his classic study of totalitarianism and collaboration, *The Captive Mind*, Milosz described how intellectuals embraced the "New Faith" of Soviet communism, with all its contradictions and cruelties, not just because they had to, but because, sooner or later, they *wanted* to. At last, an escape from the emptiness at their core:

> Would he be less dishonest if he could speak the truth?... Who knows whether it is not in man's lack of an internal core that the mysterious success of the New Faith and its charm for the intellectual lie? By subjecting man to pressure, the New Faith creates this core, or in any case, the feeling that it exists. Fear of freedom is nothing more than fear of the void.[134]

The conversion to the New Faith happened step by oh-so-easy step, as Milosz relates through the story of a writer friend he calls "Alpha," who sacrifices truth for official dogma:

> In his desire to win approbation, he had simplified his picture to conform to the wishes of the Party. One compromise leads to a second, and a third, until at last, though everything one says

may be perfectly logical, it no longer has anything in common with the flesh and blood of living people... This is the price one pays for the mental comfort dialectics affords.[135]

Humans have always been all too willing to collaborate with evil. But Milosz, like Conrad, Eliot, Orwell, and others, saw that the modern age had spawned a new species of evil, which has no origin: at its center is nothing. It's the invisible authority, punishing an unspecified crime, that arrests and executes Josef K in Franz Kafka's *The Trial*. It's the nameless monster that "slouches towards Bethlehem" in Yeats' "The Second Coming."

The Enlightenment triumph of reason helped free us from millennia of ignorance, superstition, and needless suffering. Modern democracy was one of its many gifts. But it also enabled a radical break between logic and feeling. Nazism, as I've noted, was a Counter-Enlightenment phenomenon: romanticism gone mad. But in the Nazis' mechanization of genocide, they also adopted a horrifically extreme version of Enlightenment rationalism. At his trial in Nuremburg, Luftwaffe head Herman Göring dispassionately explained the logic of bombing civilians on behalf of Franco during the Spanish Civil War. It was an opportunity to run "technical" tests of the Luftwaffe:

> The Fuehrer thought the matter over. I urged him to give support under all circumstances, firstly, in order to prevent the further spread of communism in that theater and, secondly, to test my young Luftwaffe at this opportunity in this or that technical respect... I sent a large part of my transport fleet and a number of experimental fighter units, bombers, and antiaircraft guns; and in that way I had an opportunity to ascertain, under combat conditions, whether the material was equal to the task. In order that the personnel, too, might gather a certain amount of experience, I saw to it that there was a continuous flow...[136]

The sheer, bureaucratic *blandness* of that. Reporting on the trial of Holocaust organizer Adolph Eichmann, philosopher Hannah Arendt expected to meet the Devil. Instead she was confronted with "the banality of evil." As Arendt wrote in *The New Yorker* and later in her book *Eichmann in Jerusalem,* the SS officer saw it as self-evident that he could not be guilty. He was only following orders:

The indictment implied not only that he had acted on purpose,
which he did not deny, but that he had acted out of base
motives and in full knowledge of the criminal nature of his
deeds. As for the base motives, he was sure that he was not
what he called an *innerer Schweinehund* — a dirty bastard in
the depths of his heart — and as for his conscience, he recalled
perfectly well that he would have had a bad conscience only if
he had not done what he had been ordered to do — to ship
millions of men, women, and children to their death with great
zeal and most meticulous care. This last statement, admittedly,
was hard to take. Half a dozen psychiatrists had certified
Eichmann as "normal."[137]

"Normal" has taken us to some terrible places.

For good and ill, bureaucracy is a perfect expression of the Enlightenment.
Applying rationality to government and corporate processes can make them both
more effective and more fair. But bureaucracy — rule by the organization — also
removes the human core from decision-making.

Bureaucracy realizes the hollow man at scale.

As a result, great harm has been done not only by monsters, but by
functionaries.

The catastrophe of the Vietnam War did not result from John F. Kennedy,
Lyndon Johnson, or even Richard Nixon deciding to do evil. It was the awful
result of logic, followed step by step.

Managing it were *The Best and the Brightest,* as journalist David Halberstam
dubbed them in his 1972 book of that name. They were impressive people,
recruited from top universities and corporations, led by Secretary of Defense
Robert McNamara. McNamara was the former president of the Ford Motor
Corporation and during World War II had been a pioneer of using data to plan
bombing missions. He brought the same approach to managing the war in
Vietnam. Halberstam described the impact of McNamara's formidable intellect:

…The mind was mathematical, analytical, bringing order and
reason out of chaos. Always reason. And reason supported by
facts, by statistics — he could prove his rationality with facts,
intimidate others. He was marvelous with charts and statistics...
No wonder his reputation grew; others were in awe.[138]

Still, not everyone was a convert to the quantification of leadership. After a newly-elected Vice President Lyndon Johnson raved about the brilliance of McNamara and the rest of the Kennedy cabinet to veteran Senator Sam Rayburn, Rayburn replied, "Well, Lyndon, you may be right and they may be every bit as intelligent as you say, but I'd feel a whole lot better about them if just one of them had run for sheriff once."[139]

Rayburn was prescient. McNamara's strategy for the Vietnam War was based on tragic hubris: his belief that data could win a war against a nationalist insurgency. It turned out the data didn't measure what mattered.

The commitment of the opposing forces, and their support among the population against the corrupt South Vietnamese government, would outmatch even the military might of the United States, as it had that of France in the Indochina War. Unable to claim and hold territory, let alone hearts and minds, U.S. forces resorted to measuring "success" in terms of body count. In Ken Burns' documentary TV series *The Vietnam War,* military historian Gen. James Willbanks defines the grisly absurdity of that practice:

> The problem with the war, as it often is, are the metrics. It is a situation where if you can't count what's important, you make what you can count important. So in this particular case, what you could count was dead enemy bodies.[140]

Many of those bodies had been noncombatants. By reducing all of them to numbers, by which commanders kept score, the body count incentivized the killing of civilians. As in Kafka's *The Trial,* you would not be able to find anyone who had ordered that civilians should be killed, or any reason why those civilians should die. The numbers made it happen — after people had designed a system in which numbers *could* make it happen.

McNamara ended up recognizing how wrong it all was, but far too late. Halberstam wrote:

> …Finally, when the mathematical version of sanity did not work out, when it turned out that the computer had not fed back the right answers and had underestimated those funny little far-off men in their raggedy pajamas, he would be stricken with a profound sense of failure, and he would be, at least briefly, a shattered man. But that would come later.[141]

Unfortunately, even after Vietnam we did not learn the terrible lesson of how untethered rationality can produce inhuman results. As with Vietnam, the war in Iraq was justified by a theory: after we applied a brief burst of shock and awe to remove its dictator, a nation of mutually hostile tribes and factions would become our democratic ally. Like McNamara and his team, the neoconservatives behind this theory were highly intelligent and well-educated. They had failed to learn not only from Vietnam, but from the post-World War I creation of the tragically unstable modern Middle East — including Iraq.

Many of the people who drive such disasters, like McNamara and like most of the neoconservatives, are guilty not of malintent but of obliviousness: to the harm that can be done by an inhuman system. Some, though, understand the system all too well and set out to exploit it for their own ends, perhaps within some self-justifying philosophical framework. It's hard to say of master manipulators of bureaucracy like Dick Cheney, or Mitch McConnell, or William Barr that "They couldn't have known."

Sometimes the hollowness is within the individual. Attorney General Barr, for example, seems to be a nihilist. In a 2019 CBS interview, he was asked whether he worried about his reputation, given the heavy criticisms he's faced for distorting the law in the personal service of President Trump. Barr said:

> I am at the end of my career. Everyone dies and I am not, you
> know, I don't believe in the Homeric idea that you know,
> immortality comes by, you know, having odes sung about you
> over the centuries, you know?[142]

The State of the Union &
the State of Our Minds

T he conflict between Counter-Enlightenment and Enlightenment worldviews explains much about how we got so divided. But other factors play a role as well. Some are societal, some psychological. I'll take a brief look at them here.

Money

Even without the schism of worldviews that made Trump inevitable, our democracy would be suffering corruption by money. Elected officials, no matter how honest they may be, are forced to devote far too much of their time to raising money, and then must face inevitable pressure from donors who assume their investment will yield a return. In a 2016 CBS *60 Minutes* report on fundraising in Congress, former Rep. Rick Nolan said both parties expect newly elected members to spend 30 hours a week "dialing for dollars." Former Rep. David Jolly described being told that his first responsibility was to raise $18,000 a day for the next six months.[143]

Money has had an influence on politics for as long as both have existed. But lately, with a big assist from the Supreme Court's 2010 *Citizens United* decision, fewer, richer people have had more influence than at any time since the Gilded Age. A network of about 400 billionaires, led by the Koch Brothers, the Mercer family (backers of Breitbart, Steve Bannon, and Cambridge Analytica), and a few others, is now running a permanent campaign on the scale of a third major political party. It largely controls one of the two official major parties.

Despite Trump's promise to "drain the swamp," his administration is stocked with billionaire-backed appointees at the highest levels, and pursues billionaire-friendly policies, like disabling the Environmental Protection Agency and slashing corporate and capital gains taxes. Recently, the Koch Brothers, the Mercers, and other members of the network were behind the small but well-organized protests against the coronavirus stay-at-home orders, covered prominently by right-wing media and promoted by the president. Like the Tea Party protests, they're purportedly about liberty, and most of the participants no doubt are sincere. But getting the protesters back to working and shopping, at their own risk, happens to serve the interests of their wealthy backers.

If a free popular vote leads to one result or another, all of us should accept it as democratically legitimate, whether we like it or not. But a great many of the laws Congress enacts go against the wishes of most voters. Political Scientist Michael Barber of Brigham Young University studied how closely US Senators' positions match the preferences of voters vs. donors. Donors win:

> Who do legislators best represent? … I find that senators' preferences reflect the preferences of the average donor better than any other group. Senators from both parties are slightly more ideologically extreme than the average co-partisan in their state and those who voted for them in 2012. Finally, senators' preferences diverge dramatically from the preference of the average voter in their state. The degree of divergence is nearly as large as if voters were randomly assigned to a senator. These results show that in the case of the Senate, there is a dearth of congruence between constituents and senators — unless these constituents are those who write checks and attend fund-raisers.[144]

Earlier (in "We're Throwing Our Own Party"), I referred to Jane Mayer's *Dark Money*. For understanding the distorting influence of money on politics, it's required, though disturbing, reading.

Our institutions

In 1978, a history and geography professor from West Georgia College went to Congress on a mission to tear it apart. He intended to seize power for the Republican Party and then, he presumed, put the institution back together again. The first stage of Congressman and then Speaker Newt Gingrich's plan

— tearing Congress apart — worked all too well. The second — putting it back together — not at all.

With advice from psychologist Frank Luntz, Gingrich introduced the practice of referring to the opposition as not just mistaken, as required by the parliamentary norm of civility, but as "sick," "corrupt," "depraved," "dangerous," and "un-American." Sadly for democracy, which depends on civility — even, and especially, among people who may detest each other personally — the habit has stuck. It's now common not just in Congress but throughout our public life.

The Gingrich era brought the normalization of extremist, anti-institutional political behavior, asymmetrically on the part of Republicans. It was documented by Congressional scholars Norman Ornstein and Thomas Mann in their 2012 book *It's Even Worse Than It Looks,* updated in 2016 as *It's Even Worse Than It Was.*[145]

There also have been Democratic politicians whose actions have undermined our institutions. For example, Lyndon Johnson's lies about the Vietnam War caused a still-prevalent loss of faith in government and the military. Bill Clinton risked the credibility of the presidency so he could have sex with a young intern in the Oval Office.

But the Republican Party seems to have decided as a body that nearly any means justify its ends. Senate Majority Leader Mitch McConnell boasts about this, and he's far from an outlier.[146] It could be that McConnell and other hyper-partisans are motivated only by a nihilistic interest in power — one can't know what's in someone's heart. I think it's as likely that Republicans have convinced themselves that fighting dirty is justified because Democrats are not just wrong, they're morally wrong.

Meanwhile, more and more voters are disillusioned with democracy itself. That loss of faith is tracked in an alarming series of studies by political scientists Yascha Mounk of Johns Hopkins University and Roberto Stefan Foa of the University of Cambridge. Since 2008, the percentage of Americans who have a negative opinion of democracy has soared from 25 percent to 55 percent.[147]

This only helps a demagogue like Trump.

Our public education system

The best schools in America are among the best in the world. But our average levels of student performance lag those found in many other developed nations, according to the authoritative Programme for International Student Assessment (PISA) run by the Organization for Economic Cooperation and Development (OECD).[148]

Civics education in the US is in tatters. On the 2016 National Assessment of Educational Progress civics exam, only 23 percent of eighth graders were rated proficient or above.[149]

The only beneficiaries of such trends are late-night comedy shows, which have made a staple of interviewing people on the street who can't answer the most basic questions about current affairs, history, or geography. Who's the Vice President? Who knows? Where's Chicago? Don't ask me!

It's tempting just to blame the schools. We should recognize, though, that in a public education system, the public has responsibilities too: supporting education not just financially, but culturally. It doesn't help that in our popular culture, expertise is often ridiculed, while ignorance is a punchline, as if it were an unavoidable foible of human nature.

No, it's a failing of a society that isn't seriously committed to education.

In my view, we long since should have realized that education is the modern defense industry and prioritized accordingly. In a knowledge-based economy, foreign powers don't need to invade our physical territory; now, the richest property is intellectual. Modern China almost never wastes money fighting wars. Why fight us if they can outsmart us?

How we decide

Earlier, I cited Daniel Kahneman's *Thinking, Fast and Slow*, in the context of how words and images can influence our thinking, independent of their meaning. That book is so insightful, and so useful in daily life, that I believe it should be part of the standard curriculum in high schools. I'll refer to it again here to talk briefly about how we make decisions, which is the book's principal theme.

Through decades of work, Kahneman and his late research partner Amos Tversky found that our minds have evolved to be bad at making many of the decisions demanded by modern life. That's largely because our brains treat thought as a scarce, precious resource. Thus we use as little of it as possible.

For example, in order to reduce "cognitive load," we use heuristics, or mental shortcuts. I've already mentioned the availability heuristic, by which we choose whichever option comes to mind most easily. Another example is the use of one data point to make a complex decision. A simple example is always buying the same brand of jam. The range of choices in a typical American supermarket is huge, and having a favorite brand saves much mental effort.[150]

We often use heuristics in political decisions. Policies are complicated, and comparing multiple policies among multiple candidates can involve thousands of variables. So instead, we may pick just one thing we like or dislike about a candidate, and that's that. "He's too old." "I don't like her voice." "He had me until he said X."

Candidates must be hyper-vigilant to avoid giving voters an easy out like this. When (during the 2008 primary) Barack Obama referred to rural white voters who "cling" to guns and religion, he was not dismissing those voters, he actually was counseling liberals *not* to do that, but to empathize with rural whites' values, traditions, and concerns. I know, because I was one of many campaign workers scrambling to deal with the fallout from his accidental use of the condescending-sounding "cling," and I researched it.[151]

Mitt Romney got into the same kind of trouble in 2012 by referring to 47 percent of the country as "takers."

Hillary Clinton gave handy heuristics to both the left and the right. For example, progressives could strike her off their list because she delivered highly-paid speeches to Goldman Sachs. Republicans, including some who might have been uncomfortable with Trump, could seize on her ill-considered use of a private email server, which made "Crooked Hillary" sound more plausible.

I suspect heuristics are also part of the reason for what seems like the epidemic, across the ideological spectrum, of people choosing hate over debate. As the world gets ever more complicated, despising someone can make life easier, at least cognitively. You decide they're evil, and you're done with them. Much less work.

Cognitive Dissonance

If we hold mutually contradictory beliefs, it causes us emotional stress. To eliminate that feeling, we will reconcile those beliefs — even if it requires reinventing reality.

Psychologist Leon Festinger was the first to identify this as "cognitive dissonance," in 1957.[152] Subsequent research, including recent brain imaging studies, has borne out Festinger's theory.

The power of cognitive dissonance is hard to overstate. One way that Festinger explored it was by joining a cult whose members believed the world would end early on Dec. 21, 1954. On the night of the 20th, they gathered at the Chicago home of their leader, Dorothy Martin, expecting to be rescued by a UFO from the planet Clarion. When, to their shock, the aliens failed to appear and the next day dawned as normal, they didn't conclude they must have been wrong. Instead, they agreed on another explanation, one that would spare them from cognitive dissonance: their collective presence had "spread so much light" that at the last minute, God had spared the Earth.

Most if not all of Donald Trump's supporters sincerely believe they are good people. When confronted with evidence of his racism, corruption, authoritarianism, or incompetence, they are put in a state of cognitive dissonance, which must be resolved. For example, "I'm not a racist, and I wouldn't support a racist. Therefore Trump can't be a racist." This requires ignoring or reinterpreting his birtherism, his lying and fear-mongering about immigrants, his disdain for "shithole countries," his excuses for the Charlottesville Nazis, his defense of the Confederate flag, and much more.

The conflict between beliefs and evidence is too painful, and so the evidence must be wrong. The explanation for Trump's apparent unfitness must be that the entire mainstream news industry is fake — and so are conservative outlets when they don't back Trump — or that science is bunk, or that renowned military leaders are liars and losers, or that his own government has been conspiring against him — including so many senior staff he has hired personally.

Or that it would all be fine, "if only he didn't tweet."

It isn't just Trump supporters who do this; everyone is prone to it. For example, think of those liberals who claim they're committed to affordable housing, yet somehow never vote for any measure that would make it possible, and convince themselves the only reason is their concern for the environment.

Shame

The feeling that makes cognitive dissonance unbearable is shame. It's no accident that con artists long since learned to exploit that feeling, as Trump does.

In her 2016 book *The Confidence Game,* writer Maria Konnikova explains the usefulness of shame — other people's — to a con artist:

> According to a recent study from the AARP, only 37 percent of victims older than fifty-five will admit to having fallen for a con; just over half of those under fifty-five do so. No one wants to admit to having been duped. Most con artists don't ever come to trial: they simply aren't brought to the authorities to begin with. No matter the medium or the guise, cons, at their core, are united by the same basic principles — principles that rest on the manipulation of belief. Cons go unreported — indeed, undetected — because none of us want to admit that our basic beliefs could be wrong.[153]

Shame is so painful that we prefer almost anything to feeling it. Psychoanalyst Mary Lamia described its impact in a 2011 article in *Psychology Today*:

> Regardless of the trigger, when shame is experienced the deterioration of an esteemed sense of self can be devastating. In addition to the typical emotions that can accompany shame, such as envy, anger, rage, and anxiety, we can also include sadness, depression, depletion, loneliness, and emptiness as a result. And this is where shame can become a dangerous emotion. When shame results in self-attack, it is overwhelming, and it can negatively color how you view yourself and how you assess the prospect of recovering your self-esteem.[154]

I'll just note this in passing because it's speculative, but there's a symmetry here between Trump and his marks. Trump talks and acts just the way you'd expect from someone who suffered terrible shame as a child, as in his constant need to be seen as a winner, and the satisfaction he apparently takes in mocking "losers." Along with parental hyper-attentiveness, humiliation is a potential cause of narcissistic personality disorder. While he's exploiting shame in others, Trump may be fleeing his own.

The need to believe

Another reason we're vulnerable to being conned, and reluctant to admit that we have been, because we want so badly to believe, whether it's to make sense of life or to find hope in a better future. Konnikova explains:

> That's why psychics are so dangerous: no matter what, it can be difficult to convince people that they aren't real. One former mentalist I spoke with — a magician who performs mind reading tricks instead of the usual visual illusions — ended up quitting the business. No matter her disclaimers, no matter how often she told her audience that these were all tricks, some believed even more the more she denied. In the end, she said, her conscience couldn't allow it.
>
> Harry Houdini spent the later part of his life going after psychics and mystics; he, too, felt that they were a danger beyond the simple criminal… Mysticism, he argued, was a game as powerful as it was dangerous. "It is perfectly rational to suppose that I may be deceived once or twice by a new illusion," he wrote, "but if my mind, which has been so keenly trained for years to invent mysterious effects, can be deceived, how much more susceptible must the ordinary observer be."[155]

Shady preachers, phony spiritualists, cult leaders, quack healers, get-rich-quick schemers, and other grifters are all drawn to people who, for their various reasons, need to believe.

Motivated Reasoning

Much as we like to think our beliefs are based on sound reasoning, the reverse is often true: we use reason to justify our beliefs. It happens because of the psychological factors I've been discussing here, or out of simple self-interest — hence Upton Sinclair's comment about the link between understanding and salary.

The Cornell psychologist Thomas Gilovich describes motivated reasoning as the difference between "Must I believe this?" and "Can I believe this?"[156] If we're really open to finding the truth, we'll believe what the evidence says we must believe. If not, we just go looking for anything that indicates we *can* believe what we *want* to believe.

How many of us diligently seek out information that challenges our opinions? The Founders hadn't heard the term, but motivated reasoning is why they believed in adversarial political and legal systems. Since it's so hard to challenge ourselves, we must ask our opponents to do it for us.

In a democracy, this is how political division is supposed to work.

Part III

What's Next

Restoration or Retribution?

As I write, we may be only a few months from the end of the Trump presidency. Or that may come more than four years from now. Either way, what we're going through won't be over. Trump didn't divide us into the two nations and his departure won't reunite us.

For a start, when Trump goes, he will carry the loyalty of millions of Americans with him. Loyalty, so central to the Counter-Enlightenment worldview, can be an admirable quality — say, in a friend who is at your side no matter what. Indeed, one reason Counter-Enlightenment people are suspicious of Enlightenment people, and one of the many reasons Trump got elected, is what is seen as the inherent untrustworthiness of Enlightenment progressives: "If you're so committed to change, how do we know what you stand for from one day to the next?" But when loyalty is absolute, it takes on a darker aspect. The Confederacy, as we have seen so recently, still has its defenders.

So will Trump. After all, one of his closest allies, Roger Stone, has a giant Nixon tattoo on his back.

But the greater and more lasting challenge may well come, not from those who stick with Trump, but from those who abandon him — and from those of us who rejected him from the start.

That's because after any period during which a country has sunk so far below its stated values, there is a period of shame — and reaction to shame.

Some former Trump loyalists, after one too many of his failures and betrayals, will finally recognize his unworthiness of their trust. His fatally bungled pandemic response, for example, is not just a fact, which loyalists might deny, but a phenomenon they may well have experienced in their own lives at great cost. It is also a powerful symbol of failed leadership: careless incompetence leading to the deaths of thousands of his followers. Imagine soldiers on a medieval battlefield watching their king trip over his feet while running from the enemy. Their loyalty might have withstood any challenge, except this.

For others, loyalty will have nothing to do with it. Many in Trump's own notoriously leaky administration, as well as in a Republican Congress stocked with his former opponents, have been keeping a weather eye on the polls all along. They've long since been ready to rush the lifeboats as soon as the time comes.

Still others will have opposed Trumpism sincerely, but only within their own minds, having never spoken up.

Whether they be disillusioned loyalists, cynical collaborators, or silent compliers, most will write new personal histories. Some will say no one could have known — look at what was in their favorite media every day, and what all their friends were saying! Some, including more than a few with books to sell, will "reveal" that they were resisters the whole time, doing their heroic best to protect democracy from even worse. "Anonymous" may step from the shadows, finally and too late.

We will hear echoes of 1944, when the liberation of France brought a miraculous discovery: nearly the entire nation had resisted the German Occupation.

"Paris liberated! Liberated by itself, liberated by its people with the help of the French armies, with the support and the help of all France, of the France that fights, of the only France, of the real France, of the eternal France!" proclaimed General Charles de Gaulle in his victory speech.[157]

It was an inspiring story of courage and resolve. If only it had been true.

But no. The tale of near-universal resistance was a comforting fiction, hiding the painful reality that while there certainly had been heroic resisters, most of the French had been *attentistes*. They chose to "wait and see," even as their neighbors were being taken away. Many had actively collaborated.

Wait — what? Surely I've overstepped here. Whatever we may think of Trumpism, we can't compare it to Nazism.

I agree, but only partly. We *should* be very cautious in making comparisons to one of history's most brutal regimes. But that is because we must avoid trivializing the suffering of the victims, not because all such comparisons are invalid. On the contrary, it's never more important to recognize historical parallels than before it's too late. And "too late" doesn't have to mean another Holocaust is coming. The end of democracy certainly could be. As Madison warned us in *Federalist 10*, most democracies have been "short in their lives."

So yes, as with the Third Reich, or the Soviet Union, or the Confederacy, the Trump era has brought abuse and accommodation, and the aftermath will bring shame and reaction to shame.

After Trump is gone, those who end up on the right side of history will be sorely tempted to seek retribution, as the French did after the Occupation, exposing and punishing selected, sacrificial collaborators. As human beings, we are driven to convert our shame into blame, which we cast onto others. We punish them to purge ourselves, in a ritual that was ancient at the Crucifixion — and that has no end. To the Romans, Jesus was a criminal. To Christians he was an innocent victim, dying for humanity's sins. Then Christians decided the Jews were the criminals — choosing to forget that the early Christians, including Jesus, were Jews.

No matter who is punished, evil persists. Shame and blame are mirror images of each other. Both only create more suffering.

So however satisfying it may feel to try make Trump supporters pay, it will be hopeless. What we have seen in them is not unique to them. Throughout history, collaboration has been commonplace. Under varying circumstances, to varying degrees, all of us are capable of it. It happens every day. Maybe on an occasion as mundane as a meeting at work, you'll see one brave person speak up for what's right, while everyone else — possibly including you? — plays it safe and stays silent.

Whether we flee the demon or chase it, we find in the end that it's in all of us.

I'm not saying that I think Trump's actions have been remotely acceptable, or that his supporters haven't been, at best, seriously mistaken. And yes, we must always seek justice.

But justice can be retributive, or restorative. We can punish people, or we can rebuild democracy.

That means that before we judge, we must become aware.

It took the French until 1981 to confront the truth about not just a few of them, but most of them. That was when film-maker Marcel Ophüls' quietly harrowing documentary *The Sorrow and the Pity* was finally broadcast in France, after having been banned there since its 1969 completion (except for one Paris showing in 1971).

The film intercuts first-person accounts by a few brave resisters with those of others who struggle to explain, even to themselves, their complicity with the Nazis.

"There was one value that we all shared, and that was caution," offers one.

"I'm trying to remember, but I can't," says another.[158]

But the archives did remember. Historian Thomas Paxton studied them exhaustively and published his findings in 1971's *Vichy France: Old Guard and New Order, 1940-1944*, a history of the Vichy regime under Marshal Philippe Pétain. Paxton reported that most people had aligned with whomever was in power, pivoting after the 1942 Allied landing in French North Africa:

> A crude graph of French public opinion from 1940 to 1944 would show nearly universal acceptance of Marshal Pétain in June 1940 and nearly universal acceptance of General de Gaulle in August 1944, with the two lines, one declining and the other rising, intersecting some time after... November 1942.[159]

It's popular to scorn and mock the wartime French. A supposed French propensity for surrender has become a stock joke — one that ignores World War I and much other history. But who are we Americans to laugh? To speak out against the German occupation was to risk torture and death. To speak out against Trump has required only the risk of embarrassment, strained relationships, or perhaps the loss of some business.

Before we judge the Vichy French, we must ask ourselves if we can honestly say we would have done better. With the answer in doubt, their warning should ring all the louder in our ears, as should all the warnings history has sounded.

Everything we have seen under Trump has been enabled by division. That division springs from mutual, and individual, incomprehension, whether accidental or deliberate.

After Trump, whether that time comes soon or later, many Americans will still be living within separate, limited worldviews, often fearing and even hating each other. The next president will not be able to fix that by himself. All of us who want to heal the division will be called upon to work towards that goal within our families, our communities, and ourselves.

I'll turn next to how we can.

Stop Making Sense

S o what to do?

For going on three centuries, we've been living in a post-Enlightenment world, but reason hasn't replaced faith. Facts haven't replaced feelings. The social contract hasn't replaced the tribe.

Both the Enlightenment and the Counter-Enlightenment are active, in tension, dividing our country and often, our own minds.

In fact, the division of our country may be an expression of the division within our minds. Most people are familiar with the supposed "right-brain/left-brain" duality, one side creative, the other rational. Recent research indicates that these different ways of thinking are not really fixed in different sides of the brain, but they do co-exist.[160] Some people lean more towards the creative, associative, and subjective, and others towards the logical, linear, and objective. All brains think in both ways, and both ways of thinking are valuable.

Some people learn to connect the two. These thinkers can be intuitive, or analytical, or both, depending on what works best in the moment. A chess master, for example, may appear to be the image of rationality. But great chess players invest years of study, analysis, and practice so that they can spot patterns in an instant, and "feel" the best next sequence of moves, even though the range of possibilities exceeds any brain's logical processing power.[161] From the other side, the stereotype of a jazz musician is as a purely intuitive free spirit, quite possibly one who's high. But jazz is intellectually demanding to a degree that rivals chess. Jazz expands the set of possible notes, chords, and rhythms far beyond the bounds of classical music — and jazz musicians must make musical sense out of it all in real time.

Great leaders also learn to bridge the two modes of thought. Former New York Governor Mario Cuomo often said, "We campaign in poetry, but when we're elected we're forced to govern in prose."[162] There is much truth in that, but some manage to govern in both prose and poetry. Obama was sometimes criticized for being too "professorial" in office, but he remained capable of breaking into "Amazing Grace" at a service for church members who had been killed by a racist assassin.[163] Eisenhower calmly managed the ever-shifting complexities of the Allied war effort, including volatile personalities like Patton and Montgomery, but he also had the heart to write his "In Case of Failure" letter, the night before D-Day:

> The troops, the air and the Navy did all that bravery and devotion to duty could do. If any blame or fault attaches to the attempt it is mine alone.[164]

We can all strive to bridge the divide within our own minds, and in so doing, bridge the divide in our country.

Those of us thinking within the Enlightenment worldview need to accept that our attempts at communication with the other side haven't been working. We need to try a new approach. It would be good if Counter-Enlightenment people would, too, but somebody has to start.

Communication doesn't happen when you talk; it happens when you're heard. If we're ever truly to become one democracy, we must re-learn how to talk, so that we *will* be heard.

We can start with how we use words. Let's take the classic advice of the Talking Heads, and "Stop Making Sense," at least now and then. I hope by now I've convinced you that mere sense isn't enough.

It's going to require practice. The dominance of the Enlightenment worldview has produced many generations who have been educated to think and speak in a language better suited for managing processes than forming human relationships. They've graduated from academies in which the humanities had come to be seen as more valuable if they could be scientized. Even literature ended up as "literary theory," which seems to be a form of political science — and political science assumes that politics is a science, when as actual politicians will tell you, it's also an art.

Poetry and prose.

We've come to assume that it's normal for an educated person to speak like a bureaucrat: in concepts, jargon, and logic, stripped of personality and emotion.

Consider how educated people talk about subjects that would be laden with feeling if they hadn't been safely shrink-wrapped in layers of abstraction and jargon:

Bureaucratese	Translation
prior to	before
collectively	together
cognizant of	know
problematic	wrong
equitable	fair
an individual	a person
processing	feeling

John Stuart Mill saw what bureaucracy was doing to language and to thought back in 1861:

> It must be acknowledged that a bureaucratic government has, in some important respects, greatly the advantage. It accumulates experience, acquires well-tried and well-considered traditional maxims, and makes provision for appropriate practical knowledge in those who have the actual conduct of affairs. But it is not equally favorable to individual energy of mind. The disease which afflicts bureaucratic governments, and which they usually die of, is routine. They perish by the immutability of their maxims, and, still more, by the universal law that **whatever becomes a routine loses its vital principle**, and, having no longer a mind acting within it, goes on revolving mechanically, though the work it is intended to do remains undone. A bureaucracy always tends to become a pedantocracy.[165]

We usually think of language as a tool we use to express ourselves. But language also shapes us. If you live in a world in which people habitually say "problematic" instead of the more straightforward "wrong," you start to lose the skill of knowing what you're actually feeling.

From time to time I teach classes on writing. I find I need to return again and again to the importance of "getting out of your head." If students want their writing to have an impact, they need to make their readers feel something. That requires using words that refer not to concepts but to things, actions, and feelings in the physical world, because we experience sensations and emotions not in our brains, but our bodies.

Think about how you know you're feeling afraid, angry, or loving. The sensation is in your stomach, your throat, or your heart, not your brain. Why do you feel so good when you return to a favorite place? Because of what you see, hear, and smell, not because you're explaining to yourself "why I like being here."

Feelings can only be felt subjectively, and yet educated people have been taught to use language objectively. This removes them from their own experience of the world. It's *The View From Nowhere,* in the philosopher Thomas Nagel's phrase.

In my classes, I often use a passage from Barack Obama's speech to the 2004 Democratic National Convention — words that set him on the course to the presidency. I place some of what Obama said next to a translation I've made of the same passage into the soulless bureaucratese that most of my students will have been taught to use.

Here's the soulless version:

> In America, we believe people should have physical and economic security, freedom, confidence in the rule of law, and the ability to participate in the political process.

> These are values that are shared by people of all parties, along with people who do not belong to any party. However, these values have not yet been fully realized. In this election, we must work together to make sure that they will be.

And here's Obama:

> That is the true genius of America, **a faith in the simple dreams, an insistence on small miracles.** That **we can tuck in our children at night** and know that they are fed and clothed and safe from harm. That we can say what we think, write what we think, **without hearing a sudden knock on the door.** That we can have an idea and start our own business without paying a bribe. That we can participate in the political process without fear of retribution, and that our votes will be counted—at least most of the time.[166] (Emphasis added.)

That's how you do it. That's how you reach people, even people very different from yourself, like Obama can. Because everyone can feel.

No matter what other differences we have, we probably share similar feelings. Maybe someone on one side believes strongly in gun rights and someone on the other side believes just as strongly in gun regulation, but both want their children to be safe. That's where they can connect.

We've gained so much from Enlightenment reason: science, medicine, technology, wealth, freedom from superstition and bigotry. But we also have lost so much, including the ability to feel connected with the world, each other, and even ourselves, without analysis, self-consciousness, anxiety, or irony. The Enlightenment was a re-enactment of Genesis: we ate of the Tree of Knowledge, but we have wandered in exile ever since. "After such knowledge, what forgiveness?" as Eliot asked.

We keep trying to find the way home, as Weber predicted we would. Spirituality, art, entertainment, sports, tourism, drugs — all promise a way back, though we never quite make it home to stay.

It may be that we never will. And it may be that that's OK: we may need to accept that we live in two worlds, including the two worlds within ourselves. Sometimes we need to see the view from nowhere — because facts really do matter — and sometimes we need to see the view from somewhere — because if we can't feel, we can't connect.

Nagel puts it this way:

> I want to describe a way of looking at the world and living in it that is suitable for complex beings without a naturally unified standpoint. It is based on a deliberate effort to juxtapose the internal and external or subjective and objective views at full

strength, in order to achieve unification when it is possible and to recognize clearly when it is not. Instead of a unified world view, we get the interplay of these two uneasily related types of conception, and the essentially incompletable effort to reconcile them. The transcendent impulse is both a creative and a destructive force.[167]

Often in life, the answer isn't this or that. It's both.

Across the Great Divide

All of our most divisive issues are based in our worldviews: abortion, guns, race, gender, God. If we're to have any hope of reuniting the two nations, we must learn to talk about those issues.

So far, we've failed. As I've argued here, that's because of mutual incomprehension. Our failure is exacerbated by the state of our union — what we've allowed to happen to our institutions — and the state of our minds — aspects of human psychology.

In our state of mutual incomprehension, there is no winning argument that will bring us back together.

So let's look at how it can happen differently.

As an example, I'll use what may be the most divisive issue of all: abortion rights. A milestone on our march to a Cold Civil War was the Supreme Court's *Roe v. Wade* decision of 1973. As with the Enlightenment, those on the winning side of the argument assumed it had been settled. But for those on the losing side, their values and beliefs had been dismissed by judicial fiat.

Look at how worlds collide in that moment: a legal solution to what the other side saw as a spiritual problem. There is no way to use legal language to address spiritual concerns, and vice versa. Each side thought the other was completely missing the point.

That's because each side had a different point, which they argued for in different languages, from within different worldviews.

Losing *Roe v. Wade* led anti-abortion-rights advocates to conclude that if judges could deal them such a devastating defeat, it was with judges that they must fight to defend themselves. The left had used the law to achieve great progress for its side; now the right would fight back, with abortion the most important battle of all.

In the ensuing struggle, the balance of our democracy has tilted from the voting booth to the court of law.

Today, opposition to abortion accounts for much of Trump's support, especially among people who can see what's wrong with him in every other way. For devoutly religious Christians, aborting a fetus is the same as killing a baby. If Trump gives them judges who will stop that, they'll stick with him through almost anything.

From within the Enlightenment worldview, it makes no sense that Christians would support someone whose behavior has been so un-Christian, with the lying, the cheating, and the bribing of porn stars. It didn't make sense to me, until I imagined myself into the Counter-Enlightenment worldview. This is an exercise of empathy; it requires suspending judgment about what you're seeing, and just seeing it.

Seeing the abortion-rights issue from the opposing worldview is part of it. Another is understanding what's called "vessel theology."

This is an argument, popular on the religious right, that holds that an ungodly person can be a vessel of God's will.[168] Some of Trump's Christian supporters compare him to the Persian King Cyrus, who conquered Babylon while the Hebrews were being held captive there. Cyrus freed them and directed that their Temple in Jerusalem be rebuilt. He didn't believe in the Hebrews' God, but he was a servant of God's will, and God blessed him as an anointed king.

Trump also gets compared to King David, who was beloved by God even though he was the kind of man who would sleep with a married woman, possibly against her will, and then conspire to have her husband killed in battle.

Thus some Christian Trump supporters can believe he too can be an imperfect vessel.

The liberal position on abortion is based on the Enlightenment conception of human rights: all people have a right to self-determination. Throughout history, men have controlled women, and nowhere more aggressively than in women's choices about their bodies, sex, and reproduction. From the Enlightenment point of view, if we believe in equal rights, we must support abortion rights for women.

If that's how *you* see it, I'll ask you to look at it again from within a Counter-Enlightenment worldview. Imagine that you believe deeply that when a child is conceived, a soul is created. If your response to that is, "But it's not true," you're missing my point. You're right that this belief can't be proven with facts and logic. But in the Counter-Enlightenment worldview, truth is defined by *more* than facts and logic, and if Enlightenment thinkers can't see that, they're blind to everything that matters most.

To a Christian opponent of abortion rights, abortion is homicide. If you're told that abortion is about the right to choose, what you hear is a claim that the right to choose should include the right to choose to kill. If the politicians and media you follow are telling you the American way of life is threatened by secularists who don't care about anything or anyone but themselves, what this abortion rights advocate is saying fits that story perfectly.

Now back to you as the abortion rights advocate. If you don't care about finding some way to communicate and cooperate with abortion rights opponents, you can just go on telling them they're wrong, or that they don't support equality for women. Yes, you have a right to believe they're wrong, and it's even true that some of them don't support equality for women.

But if you do want to reach them, that approach won't work. We know, because we have run this experiment over and over and over.

I've spent years advising, and learning from, leaders in politics, government, nonprofits, and the private sector, focusing on using communication strategically. That often involves managing conflict. Sometimes the conflict happens live, on-air. I frequently take part in broadcast political debates, including on conservative networks like Fox News and Newsmax, where I advocate a Democratic point of view.

I learned long ago, as did wiser people before me, that handling conflict strategically means much more than just winning a fight. In fact, fighting is the last resort. As Sun Tzu wrote in *The Art of War*, in the 5th century BCE:

> To fight and conquer in all your battles is not supreme
> excellence; supreme excellence consists in breaking the
> enemy's resistance without fighting.[169]

Fighting is too destructive, and the destruction is too hard to contain.

You can lose the war by winning the wrong battles, as King Pyrrhus learned the hard way at Heraclea and Asculum in 280 and 279 BCE. Pyrrhus ended up only winning the naming rights to the "Pyrrhic victory."

Furthermore, winning a fight fails to resolve the underlying conflict. It only defeats the opponent, which sows the resentment that will fuel the next battle. In the Civil War, the North crushed the South, but as we've seen too often, including recently in Charlottesville, the Civil War still isn't really over.

I am not saying there's never a time to fight. When the South fired on Fort Sumter, there was going to be a war. When terrorists attack, they need to be stopped. And in our politics, there are people who just need to be defeated.

But I'm not talking about that here. I'm talking about the fighting among our whole population that has split our nation in two.

There's a better way.

A strategy that works

The method I'm about to describe is based on research in communication theory and in related topics within the fields of psychology, sociology, political science, and education. I've tested it through my own experience in consulting, media, and politics.[170]

It comes down to what E.M. Forster said: "Only connect."

A good analogy is teaching. What makes a teacher exceptional is independent of any particular theory of education or set of classroom skills, or even mastery of the subject at hand, as important as all of those are: It's the ability to show students that you see them and care about them.[171]

Establish a connection and build from there.

There are five elements:

1. Greet, showing friendliness, respect — and vulnerability.
2. Pursue awareness, not judgment.
3. Find agreement on values.
4. Build trust instead of arguments.
5. Connect.

1. Greet

It's no accident that all cultures have greeting rituals. When people meet, they need to establish at least some minimum level of trust — "Is this a friend or a foe?" — and some basis on which to decide whether to continue having anything to do with each other.

All effective greetings involve the elements of *respect, friendliness, and vulnerability.*

Respect is a recognition of the status of the two people greeting each other. In hierarchical situations, it's important to recognize who's dominant. In encounters between equals, it's important to show that neither person is going to *act* as if they're dominant. Many traditional greetings feature gestures of respect, such as bowing.

Friendliness isn't just nice. It makes further interaction possible by showing that your intentions are not hostile. This is why traditional greetings from around the world involve expressions of good will, like "Good morning," "It's good to meet you," "Peace be upon you," or *"Aloha"* (which means peace, love, compassion, and more). Physical gestures such as handshakes or kisses serve the same purpose. They also give a sense of the physical, nonverbal presence of each person.

Vulnerability is often expressed in stylized form, such as the hat tip, one source of which is the removal of a helmet by a knight. Intimacy involves showing deep vulnerability — only someone who loves you can really hurt you. Many of us have trouble showing vulnerability, because we associate it with danger. As we saw in the story from Roger Ailes' childhood, some people are trained never to be vulnerable. Such people end up with few if any close relationships.

Showing vulnerability helps greatly with making a connection. First of all, nothing makes it clearer that you intend no harm than exposing yourself to the risk of harm. Second, willingness to be vulnerable can, paradoxically, be a sign of strength. This is one reason why leaders expose themselves to crowds, even though that is a risky thing to do. And third, allowing someone to see a vulnerability — perhaps by admitting mistakes you've made — is one of the most authentic ways there is to let them get to know you — the real you. What we usually show to the world is a form of armor we've built to hide our vulnerability.[172]

2. Pursue awareness, not judgment

Remember my reference to Jonathan Haidt's *The Righteous Mind* a short while ago (in "The Evolution of Tribalism")? In that valuable book Haidt shows, based on an evolution-based theory of social psychology, how hard it is for us to avoid judging each other. But it's not impossible, and it brings great benefits. In several religions and philosophies, renouncing judgment is seen as a path to enlightenment (small "e"). For example, anyone raised in the Christian tradition has heard this lesson from Jesus:

> Judge not, that ye be not judged. For with what judgment ye
> judge, ye shall be judged: and with what measure ye mete, it
> shall be measured to you again. And why beholdest thou the
> mote that is in thy brother's eye, but considerest not the beam
> that is in thine own eye?[173]

In Buddhism, one of the practices of the Eightfold Path is Right Mindfulness, which can be understood as simple awareness of what is, as opposed to living within illusions of, and attachments to, what we think *should* be. Judging, on the other hand, brings very different results, as the Buddha said:

> Don't be judgmental about people. Don't pass judgment on
> people. Those who pass judgment on people harm
> themselves.[174]

And Socrates, too, advised an open, non-judging mind:

> Although I do not suppose that either of us knows anything
> really beautiful and good, I am better off than he is, for he
> knows nothing, and thinks that he knows; I neither know nor
> think that I know. In this latter particular, then, I seem to have
> slightly the advantage of him.[175]

Such humility seems to be a characteristic of very wise people — think of Gandhi, Einstein, or Mandela. For our purposes here, it's also highly practical. Remind yourself: Is your strategic goal to punish the wicked, or is it to make progress? Accept that people are deeply flawed, because they — we — are.

Keep your eyes on the prize.

If we start off an encounter by judging — "But you're wrong" — all that's likely to follow is a fight, with the contestants' positions only hardened afterwards.

Instead, practice simply being aware of how the other person feels. Think of their belief as just interesting, instead of something that urgently requires correction. You may feel sure that they're wrong, but you can just notice that thought (silently), and plan to get back to it later, maybe.

3. Find agreement on values

When I take part in debates with conservatives, it's rare that I agree with their *policies*, but it's also rare that I can't find agreement on *values*.

Returning to the issue of abortion rights, you probably won't be surprised to hear that everyone, left or right, globalist or populist, thinks the life of a child is precious.

That's the starting place.

You might say — with, importantly, sincere feeling — "I understand why you find abortion unthinkable. What could be more important than protecting the life of a child? I'd die to protect my children."

You haven't agreed that abortion is the same as killing a child. But you have agreed that killing a child would be awful. You don't share policies, but you share values. With most people, values count for a lot more.

4. Build trust, not arguments

Once you've established agreement on values, it can be tempting to fall back into Enlightenment mode and litigate the issue, so as to establish that the other party is, in fact, wrong.

Resist!

You almost certainly won't succeed, and even if you do, it probably won't stick. Voluminous evidence indicates that, no matter what our ideology, and no matter how smart we are, we are all prone to motivated reasoning. Overcoming that tendency requires a lot of work, including the work of building self-awareness.

But if we focus on building trust instead of winning an argument, we get the advantage of another aspect of human psychology: people trust other people more than they trust data. This is why we ask our friends for recommendations. It's why shopping websites feature customer reviews. It's why marketers hire celebrity endorsers and social media influencers. And it's why we elect leaders to run things instead of just hiring expert technocrats.

If you build trust first, your opinion will carry much more weight — whether you're right or wrong. Remember all those times the facts have contradicted Trump, and yet he has kept the trust of his supporters.

Throughout history, people have established trust not through argument, but by exchanging tokens and stories. Tokens can be physical, as in a gift or the performance of a favor, or they can be symbolic, as in representations of values that matter to both parties, like a symbol of membership in a group or religion. Stories provide windows into each other's cultures, to help build familiarity and reduce suspicion of the unknown.

Consider a simple, modern example: two strangers getting to know each other by talking about music. If they find they love some of the same songs and artists, they start trading stories about when they first heard a song or about a great show they saw… and they have a connection. A bond can form within minutes. Neither has bothered to lay out a rational argument for their favorite music, they've just named it. The songs are symbols that carry payloads of feeling and meaning.

Yes, discussing politics has higher stakes than discussing music. But how the discussions work, or don't work, is similar.

In the abortion discussion, to the extent that the participants can connect over shared values, it will be hard for them to see each other as evil.

And that is called progress. Under our present circumstances, it's progress towards restoring democracy.

5. Connect

So, *now* do we get to spring the trap and win the argument? Sorry, but no. Eyes on the prize: first we have to repair a broken relationship.

Furthermore, some arguments never can be won, and maybe shouldn't be. Intolerance, on the left as well as on the right, at the top as well as at the bottom, can only take hold if we forget that democracy is about disagreement. In a democracy, people are allowed to have different opinions — and they're even allowed to be wrong.

Although the Founders were men of ideas, they understood that human behavior was often driven by interests (although they underestimated the power of identity). The Founders' goal was not to eliminate conflict among people with differing interests, which history showed would be impossible, but to channel conflict towards compromise. Madison explained in *Federalist* 51, beginning with what has become a famous quotation:

> If men were angels, no government would be necessary. If angels were to govern men, neither external nor internal controls on government would be necessary. In framing a government which is to be administered by men over men, the great difficulty lies in this: you must first enable the government to control the governed; and in the next place oblige it to control itself. A dependence on the people is, no doubt, the primary control on the government; but experience has taught mankind the necessity of auxiliary precautions. This policy of supplying, by opposite and rival interests, the defect of better motives, might be traced through the whole system of human affairs, private as well as public. We see it particularly displayed in all the subordinate distributions of power, where the constant aim is to divide and arrange the several offices in such a manner as that each may be a check on the other that the private interest of every individual may be a sentinel over the public rights.[176]

People who are certain they're right tend to associate compromise with corruption. But certainty can be far riskier. Millennia of atrocities in the name of righteousness, whether religious or ideological, should have made that more than clear by now. Compromise is what we came up with after giving violence a chance, over and over. Compromise doesn't kill people, and it achieves more lasting progress.

Compromise is also unavoidable. No ideology can account for everything. As a formal system, ideology has something in common with mathematics, which, as Gödel showed, can never be perfectly complete.[177] Ideology will involve gaps and compromises, whether its holder recognizes them or not. Gun control advocates may find themselves cheering at the sight of Harriet Tubman carrying a concealed pistol in the movie *Harriet*. People who condemn rigid Christian fundamentalism may make allowances for rigid fundamentalisms of other faiths.

Contentious issues are usually complex, with variables across dimensions of fact and feeling. Our opinions may not always add up.

Even music, often cited as the purest of art forms, involves compromise. In Western music, the word "temperament" refers to the necessity of cheating a little on the pitch of each note, because it's only possible to play perfectly in tune in one key. So instruments are tuned to compromise a little, which makes it possible to play *mostly* in tune in any key. Compromise gives us the endless glories of harmony.

And compromise builds trust.

It's hard to hate someone you trust, and at some point, you find you can work with them. Tim Kaine is a devout Catholic who opposes abortion. And yet he was Hillary Clinton's 2016 running mate. He didn't agree with her about everything, but he could work with her.

So too in a debate between any two people about abortion, or any other divisive issue. They may never agree. But if they can form some kind of relationship based on trust, that's a step towards getting our democracy back.

A democracy is made of people. So people must connect.

Many conservatives are alarmed by what Trump is doing to democracy. Some are working to stop his re-election, going so far as to pledge to vote for a Democrat for the first time in their lives. Some of these people are my friends. I usually disagree with them on policy, but we share core values. I can work with them, and they with me.

Can you make a connection with everyone? No. Good intentions matter. There are people who are attracted to Trump because their intentions are not good, and engaging with such people is a waste of time. But by engaging with people of good faith, with whom you just disagree, you can diminish the damage to democracy caused by the bad-faith gang.

Democracy can work, if we want it to. When Benjamin Franklin was asked what kind of nation we would have, he said, "A republic, if you can keep it."[178]

America Is More Than an Idea

I n order to keep our republic, we must defend reason. Nothing I'm saying here means we should compromise our commitment to that. But if reason is to survive, it can't start and end in itself, like a Penrose staircase to nowhere.[179] All of the reasoning in the Constitution is based on a Declaration of self-evident truths.

Another way of saying "self-evident truths" is "articles of faith."

America is more than an idea. America is a story we're trying to make come true.

To tell it, we need a larger language.

We've found our way to such a language before. We've heard it from Jefferson, Lincoln, Franklin Roosevelt, John Kennedy, Martin Luther King, Jr., Ronald Reagan, and Barack Obama. All of them celebrated an America big enough to hold cultures and contracts, art and science. faith and reason.

Built from a dream, America has never been fully real, and may never be. A democracy must also hold room for doubt, so that we can question our leaders, question each other, and even question everything we think we know.

But a dream doesn't have to be real in the present to be possible in the future. A dream doesn't need to explain everything.

It just needs to show the way.

Afterword, 2020:
Campaigns Are Not Logical,
but Mythological

In a presidential campaign, we're choosing a leader, not a manager. The process has more in common with mystical, ancient rites than with reviewing resumes. It's not logical, but mythological. What we search for in a leader hasn't changed much since the beginning of history, or since before history. We look for someone who will love us, fight for us, and even die for us.

The criteria aren't based in rationality, but in instinct. What catches our interest, and ends up persuading us, is what is expressed in a facial expression, the tone of a voice, the way a body moves.

Some arresting research has been done on this phenomenon by Princeton psychologist Alexander Todorov and his associates.[180] In a series of studies, Todorov has asked subjects to rate unfamiliar political candidates based only on seeing photos of each of them for a fraction of a second. *The subjects' candidate preferences match the actual election results up to 70 percent of the time.*[181]

We shouldn't read too much into one example, but there are many others.

A useful reference is *Democracy Despite Itself* (2012), by Danny Oppenheimer, a UCLA professor of psychology and management who has collaborated with Todorov, and Mike Edwards, a writer on politics. One study they cite, conducted by University of Pennsylvania researcher J. Scott Armstrong, asked New Zealand schoolgirls to rate the faces of the 2008 US presidential primary candidates:

> Despite the fact that they had no idea who any of the candidates were, these children from the other side of the globe thought that Barack Obama and John McCain looked the most competent—correctly predicting who would win the primaries. The greatest minds in American punditry were beaten by a group of completely uninformed children.[182]

People may prefer different kinds of faces, depending on whether or not they feel endangered. Oppenheimer and Todorov ran an experiment with subjects who thought John Kerry looked caring, while George W. Bush looked competent:

> Another set of studies used complex computer algorithms to create faces that were unrecognizable, but had the defining elements of George W. Bush or John Kerry's face. Even though they didn't recognize the faces, people preferred the Bush-like face in a time of war, but preferred the Kerry-like face in a time of peace. It goes without saying that at the time of the 2004 presidential election when Bush defeated Kerry, the United States was engaged in two wars—one in Iraq and one in Afghanistan. These studies suggest that issues might actually matter in an election, just not in the way we normally think that they do.[183]

Simply being taller can make a big difference:

> From 1900 to 1980 the taller candidate won nearly 80 percent of presidential elections in the United States, and the average height of male senators and governors is above six feet tall— well above the national average of five feet, ten inches.[184]

Based on my own political consulting experience, I've come to believe that the most successful candidates combine features of the Boss and the Baby: the confidence of a boss, and the lovable openness of a baby. Look at photos of FDR, Kennedy, Reagan, Bill Clinton, or Obama interacting with voters and you'll see what I mean.

And through supervising photo shoots or taking my own photos of many candidates, I've been able to run my own, non-scientific versions of Todorov's face experiments. For example, I took thousands of photos of Barack Obama in 2008, and of Hillary Clinton in both 2008, when she was campaigning for

Obama, and 2016, when she ran for president. On paper, Hillary was at least as qualified to be president as Obama was. But, even though both of them look just fine in person, it's hard to take a bad picture of Obama, and it's hard to take a good one of Hillary. Caught in a random, fleeting moment, Obama's face is likely to express optimism, confidence, and warmth, while Hillary's is more likely to show signs of tension. I'm in no way saying this is fair — after decades of brutal political battles, I can readily imagine why Hillary might carry some stress around. I'm saying this is what the camera sees, and therefore what is likely to shape voters' instantaneous choices.

Barack Obama, Battle Creek, MI, Aug. 31, 2008.
Hope: Obama's nonverbal communication carried at least as much meaning as his words.
(Photo: the author.)

Few of us have much if any control over how our faces happen to look from one moment to the next. The lucky ones are naturally charismatic, even if they're not all that beautiful. It's a truism in the movie and fashion industries that the camera just loves some people. I often assess the odds of a candidate winning based on this and other non-verbal qualities, and to date that method has been reliable.

Candidates tend not to do well if they can't connect on a nonverbal, emotional level, but instead lead with their qualifications and policies. Think of Michael Dukakis, Bob Dole, Jack Kemp, Al Gore, John Kerry, Jeb Bush, or Hillary Clinton.

In the 2020 Democratic primaries, the capable bureaucrats and technocrats, like Elizabeth Warren, Mike Bloomberg, Amy Klobuchar, Tom Steyer, Andrew Yang, and Michael Bennet, among others, fell by the wayside.

So, too, did Bernie Sanders, although he is a special case.

On the one hand, his style is very Counter-Enlightenment. The vision of the future he paints is essentially millenarian: a new age of social justice achieved through a political revolution. And no small part of his appeal is in his nonverbal presence: an emotionally authentic combination of Prophet and cranky but adorable grandpa.

But on the other hand, is an Enlightenment hyper-rationalist. He still seems to see everything in terms of economics, as in the "working class" vs. the "billionaire class." Even at this late date, his rhetoric can sound like it's held over from his days as a student organizer in the sixties, and he can't resist pointing out that the Soviets or Castro did do some good things, like providing health care and education — technically true, but culturally tone deaf. He has trouble with culture, which I think explains his difficulties expanding his coalition beyond his base.

Joe Biden is smart and accomplished, with a substantive record, but his strengths as a candidate are almost entirely non-rational. Looking at the *content* of his communication, it's easy to find non-sequiturs and gaffes. But the *feel* works. Biden is great at connecting with people, all kinds of people, nonverbally. I've taken lots of photos of him, too, and you won't be surprised to hear that the camera loves him.

I believe Trump understands this very well, and that it's why he has shown so much fear of Biden as his opponent — to the point of getting himself impeached by trying to get foreign help with sabotaging Biden.

Mythologically, a general election campaign featuring Biden vs. Trump pits a candidate of hope vs. a candidate of fear. It's a dichotomy that's quite common among presidential candidates. Obama, Bill Clinton, and Reagan were candidates of hope — Clinton and Obama literally so, with Clinton calling himself "the boy from Hope (Arkansas)," and Obama running on Hope and Change. Trump, Nixon, and Johnson (with his famous "Daisy" ad linking Goldwater to nuclear Armageddon), are examples of candidates of fear.

Biden's near-failure, before South Carolina, actually enhances his narrative of hope: he's gone through a resurrection. And the fact that he brought his troubles on himself adds yet another mythological dimension: redemption.

Trump wanted to compete against Bernie, because he believed it would have been easy to make Bernie look scary, as an "anti-American socialist." That kind of opponent plays into the hands of a candidate of fear.

But as a talented candidate of hope, Biden operates in the Counter-Enlightenment mode just as comfortably as Trump does, and even though people can be scared into voting for a candidate of fear, if you offer them both safety and hope, most will take it.

You'll hear many pundits argue that to defeat an opponent like Trump, you have to beat him at his own game. That's only partly true. If Biden runs on reason, re-enacting once again the battle of the Enlightenment vs. the Counter-Enlightenment, Trump could win again.

But if Biden leads with his Counter-Enlightenment instincts, while preserving his Enlightenment principles, he can be our next president.

About the Author

Spencer Critchley is a writer, producer, and communications consultant with experience in journalism, film, digital media, public relations, advertising, and music, and the Managing Partner of communications consulting agency Boots Road Group.

As a consultant, he has worked for both of Barack Obama's presidential campaigns, former Congressman Sam Farr, the US Department of Labor, the University of California at Berkeley, the Monterey Jazz Festival, and many others.

As a digital media producer, his clients have included David Bowie, Moby, Santana, Britney Spears, and others while he was with Thomas Dolby's Beatnik Inc; the Silicon Graphics-Time Warner-ATT interactive TV system; Silicon Gaming; and the multiple award-winning Choosing Success multimedia program for CCC/Viacom, described by Wired magazine as "the most inspired piece of educational software ever created."

As a journalist, he reported stories for the Canadian Broadcasting Corporation, National Public Radio, the Associated Press, and others, winning awards for investigative reporting from the AP and Public Radio News Directors Inc. His reporting exposed a cult operating in eight US states, and human rights abuses and murders in post-Gulf War Kuwait.

For CBC Radio, he was a correspondent and guest host for the national entertainment and popular culture show *Prime Time,* the host of the syndicated *Canada Rocks* record review, and a contributor to *The Entertainers* and other programs. He has written for HuffPost, Business Insider, the Stanford Social Innovation Review, the Toronto Star, and other publications, and is the host of the *Dastardly Cleverness in the Service of Good* podcast.

As a composer and music producer, he was signed to Warner-Chappell Music Publishing. He created music for the CBC including for the Peabody Award-winning radio drama *Paris from Wilde to Morrison* and the series shows *Prime Time, Radio Banned,* and *Metro Morning.* He composed the score (with collaborator Marco D'Ambrosio) and produced the music, dialog, and sound design for the Emmy-winning PBS documentary *Blink.*

Spencer is an adjunct lecturer in Journalism for the Middlebury Institute of International Studies. He has been a guest speaker for Stanford University's documentary film program; the American Film Institute, New York University's Tisch School of the Arts; Art Center College of Design; California State University Monterey Bay; the American Constitution Society; MacWorld; Intel Developer World; the Game Developer's Conference (GDC); Interpret America; the New Teacher Center; the California Association of Public Information Officials; and the SXSW, Hot Springs, and Bermuda Film Festivals.

He has been interviewed or quoted by ABC News, the AP, the CBC, CBS Radio, the Christian Science Monitor, Deutsche Welle, Fox News, The Hill, ITV (UK), the Los Angeles Times, NBC, Sky News (UK), USA Today, and others.

Web: spencercritchley.com
Twitter: @scritchley
Facebook: spencer.critchley.page
Dastardly Cleverness in the Service of Good: dastardlycleverness.com

Endnotes

[1] Spencer Critchley, "A Letter to a Friend Who Voted for Trump," *Huffington Post (now HuffPost),* Nov. 11, 2016, at www.huffpost.com/entry/a-letter-to-a-friend-who-voted-for-trump_b_58262fa5e4b0852d9ec215f6.

[2] Margaret Thatcher, "Speech at Hoover Institution Lunch." Hoover Institution, March 8, 1991. Margaret Thatcher Foundation: www.margaretthatcher.org/document/108264.

[3] Plato. *The Republic,* Book VI, trans. B. Jowett, Project Gutenberg, last modified June 22, 2016, www.gutenberg.org/files/1497/1497-h/1497-h.htm.

[4] : "What has Athens to do with Jerusalem?" Tertullian, *De praescriptione haereticorum (On the prescription of heretics, ca. 190-220 CE),* Tertullian.org, accessed at www.tertullian.org/works/de_praescriptione_haereticorum.htm.

[5] Thomas Jefferson to François D'Ivernois, Feb. 6 1795, US National Archives, https://founders.archives.gov/documents/Jefferson/01-28-02-0196.

[6] John Locke, *Two Treatises of Government,* Book II, 1763. Project Gutenberg, www.gutenberg.org/files/7370/7370-h/7370-h.htm.

[7] Declaration of Independence, 1776.

[8] Isaiah Berlin, "The Counter-Enlightenment," 1973, Isaiah Berlin Virtual Library, accessed at http://berlin.wolf.ox.ac.uk/published_works/ac/counter-enlightenment.pdf (PDF).

[9] Giambattista Vico, *The New Science (Scienza Nuova),* Element I, §120. Quoted in Timothy Costelloe, "Giambattista Vico", *The Stanford Encyclopedia of Philosophy* (Fall 2018 Edition), Edward N. Zalta (ed.), accessed at https://plato.stanford.edu/archives/fall2018/entries/vico.

[10] *Ibid.,* Element II, §122.

[11] Johann Georg Hamann. *Sämtliche Werken,* ed. Josef Nadler (Vienna: Verlag Herder, 1949-1957), vol. 2, 197. Quoted in Gwen Griffith-Dickson, "Johann Georg Hamann," *The Stanford Encyclopedia of Philosophy* (Fall 2017 Edition), ed. Edward N. Zalta, accessed at https://plato.stanford.edu/archives/fall2017/entries/hamann.

[12] Johann Georg Hamann, *Briefwechsel,* ed. Walther Ziesemer and Arthur Henkel (Wiesbaden/ Frankfurt: Insel Verlag, 1955–1975), vol. 7, 165. Quoted in Griffith-Dickson, *ibid.*

[13] *Ibid.*

[14] Jean-Jacques Rousseau, *The Social Contract and Discourses by Jean Jacques Rousseau*, transl. G.D.H. Cole (London: J.M. Dent and Sons, 1913), accessed at Constitution Society, www.constitution.org/jjr/socon.htm.

[15] Jean-Jacques Rousseau, *Discourse on the Origin of Inequality Among Men, Part II*, *ibid.*

[16] Edmund Burke, "Reflections on the Revolution in France" (Nov. 1, 1790). Accessed at Wikisource: https://en.wikisource.org/wiki/Reflections_on_the_Revolution_in_France.

[17] Letter to Tench Coxe. June 1, 1795, accessed at www.loc.gov/exhibits/jefferson/jeffworld.html.

[18] Ernest Renan, "Qu'est-ce qu'une nation? (What Is a Nation?)," trans. Ethan Rundell (Paris: Presses-Pocket, 1992), accessed at http://ucparis.fr/files/9313/6549/9943/What_is_a_Nation.pdf.

[19] Richard Wagner. *The Ring of the Nibelung, Das Rheingold*, Scene 1, trans. John Deathridge. (New York: Penguin, 2018), 29, Kindle.

[20] Richard Wagner, trans. William Ashton Ellis, "Judaism in Music," from *The Theatre, Richard Wagner's Prose Works*, Volume 3 (1894), 79-100, accessed online at www.jrbooksonline.com/PDF_Books/JudaismInMusic.pdf.

[21] "In extracting the pure principles which [Jesus] taught, we should have to strip off the artificial vestments in which they have been muffled by priests, who have travestied them into various forms, as instruments of riches and power to themselves... There will be found remaining the most sublime and benevolent code of morals which has ever been offered to man. I have performed this operation for my own use, by cutting verse by verse out of the printed book, and arranging the matter which is evidently his, and which is as easily distinguishable as diamonds in a dunghill." — Thomas Jefferson to John Adams, Oct. 12, 1813, US National Archives, https://founders.archives.gov/documents/Jefferson/03-06-02-0431.

[22] Gregory of Nyssa, *On Ecclesiastes* 4:1, quoted in Tom Holland, *Dominion: How the Christian Revolution Remade the World* (New York: Hachette Book Group, 2019).

[23] President Andrew Jackson, "First Annual Message to Congress," Dec. 8, 1829, accessed at University of Virginia Miller Center: https://millercenter.org/the-presidency/presidential-speeches/december-8-1829-first-annual-message-congress.

[24] "The new constitution has put at rest, forever, all the agitating questions relating to our peculiar institution — African slavery as it exists amongst us — the proper status of the negro in our form of civilization. This was the immediate cause of the late rupture and present revolution." — Confederate Vice President Alexander H. Stephens, "Cornerstone Speech" (March 21, 1861), accessed at Wikisource: en.wikisource.org/wiki/Cornerstone_Speech.

[25] Summarized by Andrea Smith in "Soul Wound: The Legacy of Native American Schools," *Amnesty International Magazine*, March 26, 2007, accessed at web.archive.org/web/20121206131053/http://www.amnestyusa.org/node/87342.

[26] "After some screenings, black audience members were attacked with clubs. The Ku Klux Klan had been disbanded in 1869, but by the mid-1920's its membership was back up to four million." — Mark Cousins, *The Story of Film: An Odyssey*. London, UK: More4 Television, 2011.

[27] In *The Gay Science,* and later in the better-known *Thus Spake Zarathustra* (1883-85).

[28] William Blake, *Milton: A Poem in Two Books*, in E.R.D. MacLagan and A.G.B. Russell, eds., *The Prophetic Books of William Blake, Milton* (London: A.H. Bullen, 1907), accessed at Wikisource: en.m.wikisource.org/wiki/The_prophetic_books_of_William_Blake,_Milton

[29] An excerpt: "Let us consider the actual, worldly Jew – not the Sabbath Jew… but the everyday Jew. Let us not look for the secret of the Jew in his religion, but let us look for the secret of his religion in the real Jew. What is the secular basis of Judaism? Practical need, self-interest. What is the worldly religion of the Jew? Huckstering. What is his worldly God? Money. Money is the jealous god of Israel, in face of which no other god may exist. Money degrades all the gods of man – and turns them into commodities…" — *Karl Marx Selected Essays*, trans. H. J. Stenning (London and New York: Leonard Parsons, 1926), 40–97.

[30] The history is related in detail by David Fromkin in *A Peace to End All Peace: The Fall of the Ottoman Empire and the Creation of the Modern Middle East,* (New York: Henry Holt, 1989).

[31] F.A. Hayek, *The Road to Serfdom* (Chicago: University of Chicago Press, 1944), 67.

[32] *Ibid.,* 69.

[33] Czeslaw Milosz, "Child of Europe," 1946. PoemHunter.com: accessed at www.poemhunter.com/poem/child-of-europe.

[34] Sigmund Freud, *Civilization and Its Discontents* (New York: Penguin Books, 2001), 103.

[35] *Ibid.,* 105-106.

[36] Max Weber, "Science as a Vocation." In *The Vocation Lectures,* eds. David Owen and Tracy B. Strong (New York: Hackett Publishing, 2004), loc. 1971, Kindle.

[37] Ron Suskind, "Faith, Certainty and the Presidency of George W. Bush," *The New York Times Magazine,* Oct. 17, 2004, accessed at www.nytimes.com/2004/10/17/magazine/faith-certainty-and-the-presidency-of-george-w-bush.html

[38] "A praise poem of Ur-Namma", Black, J.A., Cunningham, G., Fluckiger-Hawker, E, Robson, E., and Zólyomi, G., *The Electronic Text Corpus of Sumerian Literature* (Oxford, 1998), accessed at www-etcsl.orient.ox.ac.uk.

[39] Pulitzer's *New York World* and Hearst's *New York Journal* both ran *The Yellow Kid* comic strip, hence "the yellow press."

[40] Quoted in Emily W. Leider, *Dark Lover: The Life and Death of Rudolph Valentino* (New York: Faber, 2003).

[41] Unknown. The Marlboro Story, 1972, British American Tobacco Records, accessed at University of California San Francisco Industry Documents Library, www.industrydocuments.ucsf.edu/docs/fkfp0025.

[42] Quoted in Lou Cannon, *President Reagan: The Role of a Lifetime* (New York: Public Affairs, 1991), 39, Kindle.

[43] John Ford, *The Man Who Shot Liberty Valance* (Hollywood: Paramount Pictures, 1962).

[44] Just two of many possible sources on how our personalities are constructed: Albert Bandura from the perspective of academic psychology, and Sam Harris from the perspectives of neuroscience and mindfulness:

    1.   Albert Bandura, *Social Learning Theory* (New York: General Learning Press, 1971).

    2.   Sam Harris, "The Self Is an Illusion," video file, posted by Big Think, Sept. 16, 2014, https://youtu.be/fajfkO_X0l0.

[45] For example, see Jessie L. Weston, *From Ritual to Romance* (1920), accessible online at www.sacred-texts.com/neu/frr

[46] Theodore H. White, "For President Kennedy: An Epilogue," *Life* magazine, Dec. 6, 1963, accessed at www.jfklibrary.org/asset-viewer/archives/THWPP/059/THWPP-059-009

[47] For more on Kennedy's straddling of the postwar divide between Democratic Party realists and idealists, see David Halberstam's classic Vietnam War history *The Best and the Brightest* (New York: Random House, 1972),

[48] Sigmund Freud, *On Narcissism. The Standard Edition of the Complete Psychological Works of Sigmund Freud, Volume XIV (1914-1916),* ed. James Strachey (London: The Hogarth Press, 1953), 91.

[49] Accessed at https://ourworldindata.org/grapher/world-gdp-over-the-last-two-millennia, Creative Commons License (CC BY-ND 4.0), https://creativecommons.org/licenses/by/4.0/legalcode.

[50] Bureau of Economic Analysis. "National Income and Product Accounts Tables: Table 1.1.6. Real GDP, accessed at https://apps.bea.gov/iTable/index.cfm.

[51] C.R. Newsom, R.P. Archer, S. Trumbetta, and I.I. Gottesman, "Changes in adolescent response patterns on the MMPI/MMPI-A across four decades," *Journal of Personality Assessment*, 2003;81(1):74–84. doi: 10.1207/S15327752JPA8101_07. 2003-99679-007. Cited in Aline Vater, et al, "Does a narcissism epidemic exist in modern western societies? Comparing narcissism and self-esteem in East and West Germany." PloS One, Vol. 13, 1 e0188287, Jan. 24, 2018, doi:10.1371/journal.pone.0188287.

[52] J.M. Twenge and W.K. Campbell, "Increases in positive self-views among high school students: birth-cohort changes in anticipated performance, self-satisfaction, self-liking, and self-competence," *Psychological Science* 2008 Nov; 19(11):1082-6. Cited in Vater, et al, 2018.

[53] The O'Jays, "Give the People What They Want," *Survival,* Philadelphia International, 1975, LP.

[54] The Kinks, "Give the People What They Want," *Give the People What They Want,* Arista, 1981, LP.

[55] Aristotle, *Rhetoric, Book 2,* Part 12, accessed at The Internet Classics Archive, http://classics.mit.edu/Aristotle/rhetoric.2.ii.html.

[56] Jeannie Suk Gersen, "How Anti-Trump Psychiatrists Are Mobilizing Behind the Twenty-Fifth Amendment," *The New Yorker,* Oct. 16, 2017, accessed at www.newyorker.com/news/news-desk/how-anti-trump-psychiatrists-are-mobilizing-behind-the-twenty-fifth-amendment.

[57] Rick Perlstein, *Nixonland: The Rise of a President and the Fracturing of America* (New York: Scribner, 2008), loc 2899, Kindle.

[58] Bill Moyers, *Moyers on America: A Journalist and His Times* (New York: The New Press, 2004).

[59] Rick Perlstein, "Exclusive: Lee Atwater's Infamous 1981 Interview on the Southern Strategy," *The Nation,* Nov. 13, 2012, accessed at www.thenation.com/article/archive/exclusive-lee-atwaters-infamous-1981-interview-southern-strategy.

[60] Joe McGinnis, *The Selling of the President* (New York: Penguin Book Group, 1969), 123.

[61] Kevin Phillips, *The Emerging Republican Majority* (New York: Doubleday, 1969).

[62] Francis Fukuyama, *The End of History and the Last Man* (New York: Free Press, 1992).

[63] The phrase was borrowed by Kennedy speechwriter Theodore Sorenson from a chamber of commerce slogan he had seen, as related in Theodore Sorenson, Counselor: A Life at the Edge of History (New York: Harper Collins Publishers, 2008), 227.

[64] Gabriel Sherman, *The Loudest Voice in the Room,* (New York: Random House, 2017), 175, Kindle.

[65] *Ibid.,* 225.

[66] Jonathan Mahler, "CNN Had a Problem. Donald Trump Solved It," *New York Times,* April 4, 2017.

[67] James Madison, *Federalist* No. 10, accessed at www.congress.gov/resources/display/content/The+Federalist+Papers#TheFederalistPapers-10

[68] *Ibid.*

[69] See Miller McPherson, Lynn Smith-Lovin, and James M Cook, "Birds of a Feather: Homophily in Social Networks," Annual Reviews, Aug., 2001, accessed at www.annualreviews.org/doi/full/10.1146/annurev.soc.27.1.415.

[70] Bill Bishop, *The Big Sort: Why the Clustering of Like-Minded America Is Tearing Us Apart* (New York: Houghton Mifflin, 2008), 5.

[71] Winston S. Churchill, *Step By Step 1936-1939*, "Armistice—Or Peace?, (New York: G. P. Putnam's Sons, 1939), 159, accessed online at *Quote Investigator,* https://quoteinvestigator.com/2017/02/07/tiger.

[72] *Ibid.* 169.

[73] Rick Santelli, "CNBC's Rick Santelli's Tea Party Rant," 4:36, YouTube, posted by The Heritage Foundation, Feb. 19, 2009, https://youtu.be/zp-Jw-5Kx8k.

[74] Darrin McMahon, *Enemies of the Enlightenment: The French Counter-Enlightenment and the Making of Modernity* (Oxford: Oxford University Press, 2002), loc. 493-501, Kindle.

[75] Richard Hofstader, "The Paranoid Style in American Politics," *Harper's* magazine, Nov. 1964, accessed at https://harpers.org/archive/1964/11/the-paranoid-style-in-american-politics

[76] Michael Barkun, *A Culture of Conspiracy: Apocalyptic Visions in Contemporary America* (Oakland, California: University of California Press, 2013), 13.

[77] Alexander Hamilton, *Federalist* No. 68, accessed at www.congress.gov/resources/display/content/The+Federalist+Papers#TheFederalistPapers-68.

[78] Testimony of Michael D. Cohen, Committee on Oversight and Reform, US House of Representatives, 116th Cong., Feb. 27, 2019, 5, accessed at www.politico.com/f/?id=00000169-2d31-dc75-affd-bfb99a790001&usg=AOvVaw2CkzDXnayEJZFuXjjKqhSn.

[79] Julie Zuzmer, "Rick Perry, under scrutiny for his Ukraine trip, says Trump is God's 'chosen one,'" *Washington Post,* Nov. 25, 2019, accessed at

www.washingtonpost.com/religion/2019/11/25/rick-perry-under-scrutiny-his-ukraine-trip-says-trump-is-gods-chosen-one.

[80] Richard Ben Cramer, *What It Takes: The Way to the White House,* (New York: Vintage Books, 1992), 616.

[81] George Orwell, "England Your England," in *The Lion and the Unicorn: Socialism and the English Genius* (London: Secker & Warburg, 1941), accessed at the Orwell Foundation, www.orwellfoundation.com/the-orwell-foundation/orwell/essays-and-other-works/the-lion-and-the-unicorn-socialism-and-the-english-genius.

[82] Winston S. Churchill, "The Finest Hour," speech to the House of Commons, June 4, 1940, accessed at *International Churchill Society,* https://winstonchurchill.org/resources/speeches/1940-the-finest-hour/we-shall-fight-on-the-beaches.

[83] Chryl Laird and Ismail White, "Why So Many Black Voters Are Democrats, Even When They Aren't Liberal," *FiveThirtyEight,* Feb. 26, 2020, accessed at https://fivethirtyeight.com/features/why-so-many-black-voters-are-democrats-even-when-they-arent-liberal.

[84] There are too many factors that affect economic performance to make a direct causal connection between who's in power and how the economy is doing, but multiple studies show that the record is better under Democrats. A good review can be found here: Kimberly Amadeo, "Democrats vs. Republicans: Which Is Better for the Economy?" *The Balance,* April 6, 2020, accessed at www.thebalance.com/democrats-vs-republicans-which-is-better-for-the-economy-4771839.

[85] Thomas Frank, *What's the Matter With Kansas?* (New York: Metropolitan Books, 2004).

[86] "The origin of the word 'haole'," *Surfer Today* magazine, accessed at www.surfertoday.com/surfing/the-origin-of-the-word-haole.

[87] Katharyn Rodeman, "Litter Did We Know," *Texas Monthly* magazine, Jan, 2011, accessed at www.texasmonthly.com/articles/litter-did-we-know.

[88] Jeffrey S. Passel and D'Vera Cohn, "Overall Number of U.S. Unauthorized Immigrants Holds Steady Since 2009, 2. State unauthorized immigrant populations." *Pew research Center,* Sept. 20, 2016, accessed at www.pewresearch.org/hispanic/2016/09/20/2-state-unauthorized-immigrant-populations.

[89] Accessible online at www.usatoday.com/story/life/entertainthis/2015/12/12/star-wars-famous-quotes-references-explained/77111728.

[90] Tom Wolfe, "The 'Me' Decade and the Third Great Awakening," *New York* magazine, April 8, 2008, accessed at https://nymag.com/news/features/45938.

[91] The Editors of Encyclopaedia Britannica, *Encyclopaedia Britannica*, s.v. "Fili,", Sept. 1, 2009, accessed at www.britannica.com/art/fili-ancient-Gaelic-poets.

[92] Daniel Kahneman, *Thinking, Fast and Slow* (New York: Farrar, Straus and Giroux, 2011), 130, Kindle.

[93] *Ibid.,* 59-60.

[94] *Ibid.,* 61.

[95] *Ibid.,* 54.

[96] For example, see David Barstow, Susanne Craig and Russ Buettner, "Trump Engaged in Suspect Tax Schemes as He Reaped Riches From His Father," *The New York Times,* Oct. 2, 2018, accessed online at www.nytimes.com/interactive/2018/10/02/us/politics/donald-trump-tax-schemes-fred-trump.html.

[97] Neil Postman, *Amusing Ourselves to Death: Public Discourse in the Age of Show Business* (New York: Penguin Books, 1985), loc. 2278-2489, Kindle.

[98] Marshall McLuhan, *Understanding Media: The Extensions of Man* (Toronto: McGraw-Hill, 1964), Part I, Chapter 1.

[99] Postman, loc. 1725.

[100] *Ibid.,* loc. 2516.

[101] The Fact Checker team, Database of President Trump's false or misleading claims, *Washington Post,* accessed online at www.washingtonpost.com/graphics/politics/trump-claims-database.

[102] Søren Kierkegaard (as Johannes Climacus), *Concluding Unscientific Postscript to Philosophical Fragments*, trans. Alastair Hannay (Cambridge: Cambridge University Press, 2009), 96.

[103] Acts 9:3-9. (King James Version).

[104] Adam Waytz, "The Psychology of Social Status," *Scientific American* magazine, Dec. 8, 2009, accessed at www.scientificamerican.com/article/the-psychology-of-social.

[105] Eli Watkins and James Gray, "'Bannon: 'Let them call you racists,'" *CNN,* March 11, 2018, accessed at www.cnn.com/2018/03/10/politics/steve-bannon-national-front/index.html.

[106] Amy Chozick, "Hillary Clinton Calls Many Trump Backers 'Deplorables,' and G.O.P. Pounces," New York Times, Sept. 10, 2016, accessed at www.nytimes.com/2016/09/11/us/politics/hillary-clinton-basket-of-deplorables.html.

[107] Sen. Amy Klobuchar, "Amy Klobuchar: We need a President for all of America," New Hampshire Union Leader, Feb 9, 2020, accessed at www.unionleader.com/opinion/amy-klobuchar-we-need-a-president-for-all-of-america/article_033f220c-d5c5-5b5b-967a-7a19ed9e5c89.html.

[108] Michael Dunlop, *The Rise of the Meritocracy* (London: Pelican Books, 1958).

[109] Cheyanne Scharbatke-Church and Diana Chigas, "Understanding Social Norms: A Reference Guide for Policy and Practice," Henry J. Leir Institute, The Fletcher School of Law and Diplomacy, Sept., 2009, accessed at https://sites.tufts.edu/ihs/social-norms-reference-guide.

[110] Robert O'Harrow Jr., "Trump swam in mob-infested waters in early years as an NYC developer," *Washington Post,* Oct. 16, 2015, accessed at www.washingtonpost.com/investigations/trump-swam-in-mob-infested-waters-in-early-years-as-an-nyc-developer/2015/10/16/3c75b918-60a3-11e5-b38e-06883aacba64_story.html.

[111] Charles Darwin, *The Descent of Man, and Selection in Relation to Sex,* Project Gutenberg, last modified Dec. 17, 2018, accessed at www.gutenberg.org/ebooks/2300.

[112] Muzafer Sherif and Carolyn W. Sherif, "Ingroup and intergroup relations." Chapter 19 in James O. Whittaker (Ed.), *Introduction to Psychology* (Philadelphia: Saunders, 1965).

[113] Jonathan Haidt, *The Righteous Mind: Why Good People Are Divided by Politics and Religion* (New York: Pantheon Books, 2012), loc. 79, 121, Kindle.

[114] "Why Do We Vote the Way We Do? New Findings Hold Surprises," *Dastardly Cleverness in the Service of Good* podcast, Feb. 26, 2018, starting at 2:12, accessed at https://dastardlycleverness.com/why-do-we-vote-the-way-we-do-new-findings-hold-surprises.

[115] M. Galesic, W. Bruine de Bruin, M. Dumas, A. Kapteyn, J. E. Darling and E. Meijer, "Asking about social circles improves election predictions," *Nature Human Behavior* 2, ,Feb. 26, 2018, 187–193, accessed at www.nature.com/articles/s41562-018-0302-y.

[116] Rob Moynihan, "'The Tribe Has Spoken': The Story Behind Survivor's Iconic Catchphrase," *TV Insider,* Feb. 24, 2015, accessed at www.tvinsider.com/1553/the-tribe-has-spoken-the-story-behind-survivors-iconic-catchphrase.

[117] *Ibid.,* loc 1961.

[118] Max Weber, "Politics as a Vocation." In *The Vocation Lectures,* eds. David Owen and Tracy B. Strong (New York: Hackett Publishing, 2004), loc. 2117, Kindle.

[119] Natasha Bertrand and Darren Samuelsohn, "What if Trump won't accept 2020 defeat?" *Politico,* June 21, 2019, accessed at www.politico.com/story/2019/06/21/trump-election-2020-1374589.

[120] The post-9/11 creation of the US Department of Homeland Security was an organizational decision, based on the need to coordinate multi-dimensional security challenges across the bureaucracy. But its name also represented a cultural shift, in the direction of the Counter-Enlightenment. At the time, I thought that the name sounded jarring in the American context, because of my Enlightenment-based belief that America is an idea, not a homeland. I didn't appreciate how pervasive the Counter-

Enlightenment worldview still was, or how much better that word would sound to Americans living within that worldview, especially with the nation under attack. I saw a civic nation under attack, they, an ethnic one.

[121] Erin Durkin and Darren Samuelsohn, "Trump lawyer: Trump can't be prosecuted for shooting someone," *Politico,* Oct. 23, 2019, accessed at www.politico.com/news/2019/10/23/trump-lawyer-prosecuted-shooting-someone-055648.

[122] Meagan Flynn and Allyson Chiu, "Trump says his 'authority is total.' Constitutional experts have 'no idea' where he got that." *Washington Post,* April 14, 2020, accessed at www.washingtonpost.com/nation/2020/04/14/trump-power-constitution-coronavirus.

[123] Michael Brice-Saddler, "While bemoaning Mueller probe, Trump falsely says the Constitution gives him 'the right to do whatever I want'," *Washington Post,* July 23, 2019, accessed at www.washingtonpost.com/politics/2019/07/23/trump-falsely-tells-auditorium-full-teens-constitution-gives-him-right-do-whatever-i-want.

[124] Accessed at *Quote Investigator*, https://quoteinvestigator.com/2017/11/30/salary.

[125] Mario Carrasco, "Progressive Latino pollster: 98% of Latinos do not identify with 'Latinx' label," *Medium,* Nov. 2, 2019, accessed at https://medium.com/@ThinkNowTweets/progressive-latino-pollster-trust-me-latinos-do-not-identify-with-latinx-63229adebcea.

[126] John McWhorter, "Why Latinx Can't Catch On," *The Atlantic,* Dec. 23, 2019, accessed at www.theatlantic.com/ideas/archive/2019/12/why-latinx-cant-catch-on/603943.

[127] Adam Serwer, "The Cruelty Is the Point," *The Atlantic,* Oct. 3, 2018, accessed at www.theatlantic.com/ideas/archive/2018/10/the-cruelty-is-the-point/572104.

[128] Tom Holland, *Dominion: How the Christian Revolution Remade the World* (New York: Hachette Book Group, 2019).

[129] *Enuma Elish,* Tablet VI, 93-109, accessed at www.ancient.eu/article/225/enuma-elish---the-babylonian-epic-of-creation---fu.

[130] In *De Cive* (1642) and again in *Leviathan* (1651).

[131] Rena L. Repetti, Shelley E. Taylor, Teresa E. Seeman, "Risky families: family social environments and the mental and physical health of offspring," *Psychological Bulletin,* 2002, accessed at https://pdfs.semanticscholar.org/b8d9/c345fe88357eecbab6a716b10488e31edef3.pdf.

[132] Mary L. Trump, *Too Much and Never Enough: How My Family Created the World's Most Dangerous Man* (New York: Simon & Schuster, 2020), pages 25-26, Kindle.

[133] Paul Schwartzman and Michael E. Miller, "Confident. Incorrigible. Bully: Little Donny was a lot like candidate Donald Trump," in *Trump Revealed,* (New York:

Scribner, Simon & Schuster, 2016), accessed at www.washingtonpost.com/lifestyle/style/young-donald-trump-military-school/2016/06/22/f0b3b164-317c-11e6-8758-d58e76e11b12_story.html.

[134] Czeslaw Milosz, trans. Jane Zielonko,*The Captive Mind* (New York: Knopf, 1953).

[135] *Ibid.,*

[136] International Military Tribunal, *Nuremberg Trial Proceedings, Vol. 9,* "Eightieth Day, Wednesday, 13 March 1946," accessed at https://avalon.law.yale.edu/imt/03-13-46.asp#Goering1.

[137] Hannah Arendt, "Eichmann in Jerusalem," *The New Yorker,* Fe. 8, 1963, accessed at www.newyorker.com/magazine/1963/02/16/eichmann-in-jerusalem-i.

[138] David Halberstam, *The Best and the Brightest,* (New York: Modern Library, 2001), page 248, Kindle.

[139] *Ibid.,* loc 262.

[140] *The Vietnam War: Resolve (January 1966 — June 1967).* Directed by Ken Burns. Walpole, NH: Florentine Films, 2017.

[141] Halberstam, page 248.

[142] *CBS This Morning,* "Attorney General William Barr on caring about his reputation: 'Everyone dies'," *CBS News,* 6:21, May 31, 2019, accessed at www.cbsnews.com/news/william-barr-interview-attorney-general-on-caring-about-his-reputation-everyone-dies-exclusive.

[143] Norah O'Donnell, "Dialing for Dollars," CBS News' *60 Minutes,*, April 24, 2016, accessed at www.cbsnews.com/news/60-minutes-are-members-of-congress-becoming-telemarketers.

[144] Michael J. Barber, "Representing the preferences of donors, partisans, and voters in the US Senate," *Public Opinion Quarterly,* Volume 80, Issue S1, Jan. 1, 2016, 225-249, accessed online at http://michaeljaybarber.com/s/POQ_Early_Access.pdf.

[145] Thomas E. Mann and Norman J. Ornstein, *It's Even Worse Than It Was: How the American Constitutional System Collided with the New Politics of Extremism* (New York: Basic Books, 2016).

[146] Kelsey Snell, "McConnell: 'I'm Not Impartial' About Impeachment," NPR, Dec. 17, 2019, accessed at https://www.npr.org/2019/12/17/788924966/mcconnell-i-m-not-impartial-about-impeachment.

[147] Yascha Mounk and Roberto Stefan Foa, "This Is How Democracy Dies," The Atlantic magazine, Jan. 29, 2020, accessed at www.theatlantic.com/ideas/archive/2020/01/confidence-democracy-lowest-point-record/605686.

[148] Programme for International Student Assessment, PISA 2018 Results," accessed at www.oecd.org/pisa/publications/pisa-2018-results.htm.

[149] Sarah Shapiro and Catherine Brown, "The State of Civics Education," Center for American Progress, Feb. 21, 2018, accessed at www.americanprogress.org/issues/education-k-12/reports/2018/02/21/446857/state-civics-education

[150] An often-cited 2000 study found that even though we might assume more choices are better, people are more likely to buy gourmet jam when offered six options rather than 24 or 30, and to be happier with their choice afterward: SheenaS. Iyengar and Mark R. Lepper, "When Choice is Demotivating: Can One Desire Too Much of a Good Thing?" *Journal of Personality and Social Psychology,* 2000, Vo7l.9, No.6, 995-1006, accessed at https://faculty.washington.edu/jdb/345/345%20Articles/Iyengar%20%26%20Lepper%20(2000).pdf.

[151] For example, see Charlie Rose, interview with Senator Barack Obama, *Charlie Rose,* PBS, Oct. 19, 2006, from 7:40 to 34:50, accessed at https://charlierose.com/videos/16337.

[152] Leon Festinger, *A Theory of Cognitive Dissonance* (Stanford: Stanford University Press, 1957).

[153] Maria Konnikova, *The Confidence Game: Why We Fall for It… Every Time* (New York: Penguin Random House, 2017), 11, Kindle.

[154] Mary C. Lamia, Ph.D., "Shame: A Concealed, Contagious, and Dangerous Emotion," *Psychology Today,* Apr. 4, 2011, accessed at www.psychologytoday.com/us/blog/intense-emotions-and-strong-feelings/201104/shame-concealed-contagious-and-dangerous-emotion.

[155] *Ibid.,* 83.

[156] Thomas Gilovich, *How We Know What Isn't So: The Fallibility of Human Reason in Everyday Life* (New York: The Free Press, 1991).

[157] Gen. Charles DeGaulle, "But Paris Liberated!" speech. Hôtel de Ville, Paris, Aug. 25, 1944. Accessed at http://witnify.com/charles-de-gaulles-paris-liberated-speech.

[158] Marcel Ophüls, *The Sorrow and the Pity* (Germany: Norddeutscher Rundfunk, 1971).

[159] Robert O. Paxton, *Vichy France: Old Guard and New Order, 1940-1944* (New York: Alfred A. Knopf, 1972), loc 4543, Kindle.

[160] E.g. see Robert H. Shmerling, MD, "Right brain/left brain, right?" Harvard Health Publishing, updated Nov. 8, 2019, accessed at www.health.harvard.edu/blog/right-brainleft-brain-right-2017082512222.

[161] See Kahneman, Chapter 22, "Expert Intuition: When Can We Trust It?"

[162] Speech at Yale University, Feb. 15, 1985. Cited in Fred R. Shapiro, ed., *The Yale Book of Quotations* (New Haven, CT: Yale University Press, 2006), 182.

[163] "Obama Sings 'Amazing Grace'," The New York Times, June 26, 2015, accessed online at www.nytimes.com/video/us/politics/100000003766925/obama-sings-amazing-grace-.html.

[164] "In Case of Failure Message," Eisenhower's Pre-Presidential Papers, Principal File, Box 168, Butcher Diary June 28 - July 14, 1944 (2); NAID #186470, Dwight D. Eisenhower Presidential Library, accessed online at www.eisenhowerlibrary.gov/research/online-documents/world-war-ii-d-day-invasion-normandy.

[165] John Stuart Mill, *Considerations on Representative Government,* (London: Parker, Son, and Bourn, 1861), "VI – Of the Infirmities and Dangers to which Representative Government is Liable," Project Gutenberg, last modified Feb. 6, 2013, accessed at www.gutenberg.org/files/5669/5669-h/5669-h.htm.

[166] Sen. Barack Obama, "Speech to the 2004 Democratic National Convention," posted by C-SPAN, Aug. 18, 2008, accessed at https://youtu.be/eWynt87PaJ0.

[167] Thomas Nagel, *The View From Nowhere* (Oxford: Oxford University Press, 1986), 3, Kindle.

[168] Tara Isabella Burton, "The biblical story the Christian right uses to defend Trump," *Vox*, March 5, 2018, accessed at www.vox.com/identities/2018/3/5/16796892/trump-cyrus-christian-right-bible-cbn-evangelical-propaganda.

[169] Sun Tzu, *The Art of War*, III:2, Internet Classic Archive, accessed at http://classics.mit.edu/Tzu/artwar.html.

[170] "Only connect! That was the whole of her sermon. Only connect the prose and the passion, and both will be exalted, and human love will be seen at its height. Live in fragments no longer. Only connect, and the beast and the monk, robbed of the isolation that is life to either, will die." — E.M. Forster, *Howard's End* (London: Edward Arnold, 1910), Chapter 23.

[171] As I first learned from my father, David Critchley, who was an expert in this area, and from my sister, Beth Charlton, also an expert, and from *my* best teachers.

[172] I first started thinking hard about the idea of personality as armor through working on the Emmy-winning PBS documentary *Blink* (2001), directed by Elizabeth Thompson.

[173] Matthew 7:1-3. (King James Version).

[174] Anguttara Nikaya, 6.44, Anguttara Nikaya, 6.44, trans. Bhikkhu Sujato, Reading Faithfully, uploaded 2018, accessed at www.readingfaithfully.org/anguttara-nikaya-translated-by-bhikkhu-sujato-free-epub-kindle-pdf.

[175] Plato, *Apology,* Project Gutenberg, last modified Jan. 15, 2013, accessed at www.gutenberg.org/ebooks/1656.

[176] James Madison, *Federalist* No. 51, accessed at www.congress.gov/resources/display/content/The+Federalist+Papers#TheFederalistPapers-51.

[177] The editors of the Stanford Encyclopedia of Philosophy, "Gödel's Incompleteness Theorems," *Stanford Encyclopedia of Philosophy*, last modified Jan 20, 2015, accessed at https://plato.stanford.edu/entries/goedel-incompleteness.

[178] As recorded by Dr. James McHenry, a Constitutional Convention delegate from Maryland and published in *The American Historical Review,* vol. 11, 1906, 618. Excerpt accessed at Bartleby.com, www.bartleby.com/73/1593.html.

[179] This is sometimes called an Escher staircase, after the famous 1960 lithograph by M.C. Escher, but it was first conceived shortly before by Lionel and Roger Penrose.

[180] Christopher Y. Olivola and Alexander T. Todorov, "Elected in 100 milliseconds: Appearance-based trait inferences and voting." In: *Journal of Nonverbal Behavior*, 2010; Vol. 34, No. 2. 83-110.

[181] This does not mean that instantaneous impressions produce accurate judgments. Todorov has also done research indicating that first impressions are compelling but inaccurate. See Alexander Todorov, *Face Value: The Irresistible Influence of First Impressions.* (Princeton and Oxford: Princeton University Press, 2017).

[182] Danny Oppenheimer and Mike Edwards, *Democracy Despite Itself: Why a System That Shouldn't Work at All Works So Well* (Cambridge, Massachusetts: MIT Press, 2012), 40, Kindle.

[183] *Ibid.,* 41.

[184] *Ibid.,* 41.